SOWING A SEED OF FAITH AND HOPE

The Life and Mission of Abraham Khayesi

Meleckidzedeck Khayesi

Copyright © 2019 Meleckidzedeck Khayesi

All rights reserved.

This publication may not be reproduced, in whole or in part, by any means including photocopying or any information storage or retrieval system, without the specific and prior written permission of the publisher.

This book is sold subject to the condition that it shall not, by way of trade or otherwise, be re-sold, hired out, or otherwise circulated without the author's or publisher's prior consent in any form of binding or cover other than that in which it is published and without a similar condition including this condition being imposed on the subsequent purchaser.

First Edition: June 2019

Published by Nsemia Inc. Publishers (www.nsemia.com)

Cover Concept: Joshua Mwangangi

Cover Design: Linda Kiboma

Layout Design: Linda Kiboma

Production Consultant: Matunda Nyanchama

Note for Librarians:

A cataloguing record for this book is available from Library and Archives Canada.

ISBN: 978-1926-906-78-2

DEDICATION

To all development students, scholars, practitioners, policy makers and other potential beneficiaries, who in one way or the other, have toiled and striven to make the earth a better habitat.

TABLE OF CONTENTS

List of Tables vii

List of Figures ix

List of Boxes..ix

Preface xi

Foreword.. xiii

Acknowledgements xv

Abbreviations and Acronyms xvii

CHAPTER ONE: When you drink water, remember the source........1

CHAPTER TWO: Roots and branches..5

CHAPTER THREE: Marriage..9

CHAPTER FOUR: Conversion to Christianity....................................13

CHAPTER FIVE: Education 23

CHAPTER SIX: Beyond officially defined boundaries 27

CHAPTER SEVEN: Abraham Khayesi completes his sojourn..........43

CHAPTER EIGHT: Sabeti Shanyisa becomes baba and mama.......51

CHAPTER NINE: Lest we forget: continuing to sow the seed of faith and hope.. 63

LIST OF TABLES

Table 3.1: Children of Abraham Khayesi who survived childhood.....12

LIST OF FIGURES

Figure 2.1: Tiriki Division..5

List of boxes

Box 4.1: PAOC and PAG..16
Box 5.1: Practice of record keeping by Abraham Khayesi............25
Box 6.1: Sabeti Khayesi: multiple roles of a pastor's wife............32
Box 8.1: A great African mother...57
Box 8.2: Precious memories...58
Box 8.3: My First Christmas in Heaven...60

PREFACE

In the African society and many other societies around the world, it is common practice to tell the life stories of individuals. Eulogies are often read and chanted at funerals as well as at burial services of individuals. In some cases, the life stories of individuals are written for future and contemporary generations to learn about the positive and negative aspects of these individuals' past. There has been a long desire among the children of Abraham Khayesi to produce a book on his life for the lessons it can offer to the family and members of the society.

My father, Abraham Khayesi, died in 1973 when I was eleven years old. When the family assigned me the responsibility of writing this book, I welcomed it partly because I admire the work of my parents and partly because it helped me to learn more about them. The process of preparing this tribute has enabled me to gain deeper knowledge not just about my parents but also my local community, the Tiriki, and the Pentecostal Assemblies of God fellowship and movement in East Africa. What has intrigued me the most is the transformation of Abraham Khayesi from a young Tiriki man, who was poised for a key role in his local traditional community, to a key player in the Christian faith; promoting the establishment and expansion of Christianity in Kenya and East Africa. In him, we see not only a pastor who is devoted to evangelization but also a father, a husband, a friend, a farmer, an entrepreneur, an arbitrator, a peace-maker, an educationist and a social mentor. In him, we see an achiever who could easily have succumbed to the tendency to become proud and arrogant but instead he chose the route of humility and down-to-earth attitude, and was ready to be involved in the ordinary life issues and challenges of people in order to share the love of God and to contribute to building his community. While many men of his age and stature would not do certain things that were considered culturally inappropriate for men, Abraham Khayesi did not have any problem preparing morning tea for his family, babysitting, keeping night vigil or guard with others when neighbouring communities threatened to attack his village, and fetching water from the stream. Though highly respected in society and the Church, he had no problem working on his coffee farm, looking after his cows as well as milking them, harvesting maize and other crops, cleaning up the village water well and entertaining his colleagues, while humming his favourite Christian songs such as "Ni lidikhu liu vuyanzi" (Oh Happy Day) and "O Yesu nguyanza" (My Jesus I love you). His approach to life has inspired me deeply.

Meleckidzedeck Khayesi
May 2019

FOREWORD

The Pentecostal Assemblies of God fellowship in East Africa has grown in membership and activities. In the place of grass-thatched churches, we now have iron roofed buildings. In the place of pastors walking on foot or using the bicycle, we now have some that use motorcycles and cars to reach their distant members. Instead of a handful of assemblies, Pentecostal Assemblies of God (Kenya) (PAG) (K) has over 3,000 assemblies or churches in different counties in Kenya. The primary and secondary schools such as Nyang'ori High School, Kereri Girls High School and Goibei Girls High School, which were started by the generation of yester-years, continue to cater for the educational needs of boys and girls in Kenya. With all these developments, it is easy, as it often happens in human history, to forget about the origins and even destroy the true source of what we see and reap today as fruits. I hope that this contextualized story of Abraham Khayesi will help the reader understand, explore and preserve the importance of plain faith and simplicity in approach to Christian life that saw Abraham Khayesi and many other ordinary people share the gospel of Jesus Christ within and beyond their communities. The value of this book largely lies in helping the present and future generations to learn about the origin and the vision of the Pentecostal Assemblies of God fellowship and mission in East Africa.

John Juma
Former General Superintendent, PAG (K)

ACKNOWLEDGEMENTS

I am grateful to my family members, relatives and friends for granting me the honour to be the scribe for this great life story of Abraham Khayesi. I thank all the people and institutions that provided information, assistance, encouragement and advice during the preparation of this book. I may not be able to mention all of them here but only a few: participants in a consultative group meeting held in 2009, respondents to interviews, PAG (K) Headquarters Office, Goibei Mission Station, African Israel Nineveh Church Office at Jebrok, Zakaria Khadambi, Zachariah Samita, Isaac Shadora, John Ingosi, Kelvin Adidi, Musa Andambi, Bildad Ajanga, Marie Khanyanji, Rynah Kadasia, Felicia Yieke, Painito Ajanga, Ryan Itambo, Simon Kibagendi Omwansa, Asheri Mugadia, Johnstone Khasi Mugadia, Constance Ambasa Shisanya, Ezekiel Jengo, Joyce Kemuma, Ezekiel Alembi, Abigail Mmbone Stingo, Neville Chungani, Ruth Busolo, Margaret Khashindu, Jessica Rembo, Peter Mala, Florence Ajanga, Rosemarie Nyaranga, Fridah Khasikani, Jane Nyakecho, Zipporah Shanyisa, David Khayesi, Dolline Busolo, Esther Khadambi, John Juma, Meshack Kaina, Heinz and Edelgard Battermann, Fidelia Shisigani, Modyline Khayesi and David Omalla.

ABBREVIATIONS AND ACRONYMS

ADC	Africa Divine Church
ACHS	Africa Church of the Holy Spirit
AINC	Africa Israel Nineveh Church
COG	Church of God
CMS	Church Missionary Society
FAM	Friends Africa Mission
PAOC	Pentecostal Assemblies of Canada
PAG (K)	Pentecostal Assemblies of God (Kenya)

CHAPTER ONE
"When you drink water, remember the source"

The title of this chapter is an adage among the Asian communities, such as the Vietnamese and Chinese, which reminds us about a vital human ethical value, namely, to appreciate the source of what we have. While we may initiate changes and even achieve more, this adage is a humble reminder that we need to also think about continuity with the origins. We learn from history that there are many people who play important roles in the initiation, growth and development of any initiative, be it political, social, economic, environmental or religious. While some operate at the frontline, others work in the background. Whatever position they occupy, their contributions are important to the overall development of an initiative. The present and future generations may reap the fruit of these initiatives but may not always fully comprehend the sacrifices and the vision of the founders. This book is about the life of Abraham Khayesi, one of the key players in founding and spreading the Christian faith in Kenya through the Pentecostal Assemblies of Canada (PAOC) and the Pentecostal Assemblies of God, Kenya (PAG) (K).

Paul, an apostle in the early days of Christianity, argues that while some people plant, others water and yet others harvest at different periods in the development of the Christian faith (1 Corinthians 3: 5-10). Knowledge of the life of an individual who participated in the founding and/or expansion of Christianity can provide insights into the source of the fruits that the present and future generations may be reaping. Abraham Khayesi was among the pioneer local pastors and workers with the PAOC and PAG (K). He was actually among the first group of pastor trainees at Bethel Bible Institute at Goibei Mission Station in Kenya. He worked as a local pastor and leader with a number of missionaries from PAOC and the sister denomination, PAG (K), to establish congregations and spread the gospel of God in Tiriki, Western Kenya and Jinja in Uganda. His first wife, Maria Khanyanji, who died, and the second one, Sabeti Shanyisa, who he married thereafter, were ministers in their own right. They made important contributions to the family, the Church and the community, including supporting and working side by side with Abraham Khayesi. There are many local pastors and members of congregations who fulfilled these functions in many parts of Kenya.

Abraham Khayesi was based in Tiriki but there were many other leaders and followers of the movement based in Maragoli, Bunyore, Nyang'ori, Kisii, Kakamega, Busia, Nyanza, Nakuru, Nairobi, Mombasa, Nandi and other parts of Kenya, who pursued the same goal of spreading Christianity. The names of some of these leaders, missionaries and followers that we often heard mentioned in our family and/or interacted with are: Otto Keller, Matia Elanogwa, John Lynn, Daudi Chole, Solomon Kinambedi, Heinz Battermann, Joel Chamwada, Isaya Kayeli, Charles Gungu, Iris Scheel, Shem Irangi, Jeremiah Vogelu, Samuel Adamba, McBride, William Ngoitsi, Yakobo Ananda, Aineah Odondi, Abneal Mwevi, Eliakim Nyamboki and Yohana Ajega. Our mother, Sabeti Shanyisa, often talked about a missionary by the name Macquarie[1] whom she remembered as having drowned while swimming with other missionaries at the Kenyan coast in Mombasa. She would tell us how the wave swept him back and forth until it took him away.

In addition to the missionaries and local pastors who were mainly involved in preaching the Gospel and doing pastoral work in Churches, there were several other people who worked as teachers, administrators and health professionals. There are also many individuals who performed several roles. For example, many members of PAOC and PAG in Kenya remember Iris Scheel, a missionary who came to Kenya as a young lady and who, over the years, worked in various capacities as a Sunday school teacher, a secondary school teacher and headmistress, youth worker and director of an education centre at Goibei. Another example was Daniel Undusu, who was a teacher and later became a pastor. It can be seen that the life and mission of Abraham Khayesi is therefore only a part of a broader movement that was devoted to spreading the Christian faith in different parts of the world, and particularly in Kenya and East Africa.

Tribute

This book is the Khayesi family's tribute to their parents — Abraham Khayesi, Maria Khanyanji and Sabeti Shanyisa — whom the children, grandchildren, community members, PAOC and PAG (K) admire for their commitment to faith, role models, and service to society. As expected, they faced both fulfilling and challenging

---

[1] I have written this name as I heard it from my mother. There are several incidents in Africa in which European names were and still are pronounced using local African language accents.

moments, and trusted God and did what was within their possibility to share the love of God and their lives with many other people. Their mentoring influence has been felt not only in the Khayesi family but also in the community. The Khayesi family gives thanks to God that the work their parents contributed to, is continuing to bear fruit. Although Meleckidzedeck Khayesi is indicated as the author of this book, he is only a scribe on behalf of the entire Khayesi family and friends of these three workers. This tribute is therefore the collective work and reflection of the children, grandchildren, relatives and friends of Abraham Khayesi, Maria Khanyanji and Sabeti Shanyisa. The family counts it a privilege to have been the children and friends of these three workers of faith in God and prays that they, family members, shall continue to build on the firm foundation their parents and society laid for them.

Tracking traces of life

Gathering and analyzing information on the life of an individual, especially on one with an extensive reach as is the case in this book, is an intriguing, iterative process. Such individuals were busy pursuing their mission and might not have thought that one day, they will be the subject of research and writing. Information on such individuals tends to be spread in many places, deposited with or within several institutions and people. However, they leave traces of their lives in and with many people and places, which can be tracked and mined for writing and learning.

I utilized several sources to gather information for this book. These sources included:

- listening to and reviewing family stories and experiences of grandparents, parents, uncles, aunts, brothers, sisters, nieces and nephews. I had to check with family members for contributions about details I have heard in many stories told in the family about Abraham Khayesi, Maria Khanyanji and Sabeti Shanyisa
- listening to stories from friends and community members who knew and/or worked with Abraham Khayesi, Maria Khanyanji and Sabeti Shanyisa;
- reviewing family records, correspondence and pictures, including notebooks used by Abraham Khayesi and Sabeti Khayesi;
- holding a consultative meeting with family members, friends and local community members on 20 June 2009;

- consulting a few key resource people to fill in the gaps in information gathered; and
- reviewing some published and unpublished documents and records.

I utilized available communication modes to gather and transmit information while preparing this book. These included face-to-face meetings, e-mails, telephone, text messaging, word of mouth and postal office. A draft of the book was reviewed by family members and other resource people, including two researchers in religion and another one in education. It was revised, edited and produced. While the book has been checked for accuracy as much as possible, I do recognize that there may still be some errors in the text. While I take responsibility for such errors, I wish to request readers to inform me about any errors they may identify.

CHAPTER TWO
Roots and branches

Abraham Khayesi was born in 1907[2] in Erusui Village, Tiriki location, among the Tiriki people (see Figure 2.1). He belonged to the Abasuba clan. His father was known as Lugondi and mother was known as Khadolwa, daughter of Andeje. Lugondi was the son of Khadambi, who was the son of Nivulia, who was the son of Musuva. Lugondi's mother was known as Duvula. The mother of Duvula was known as Wiyanga.

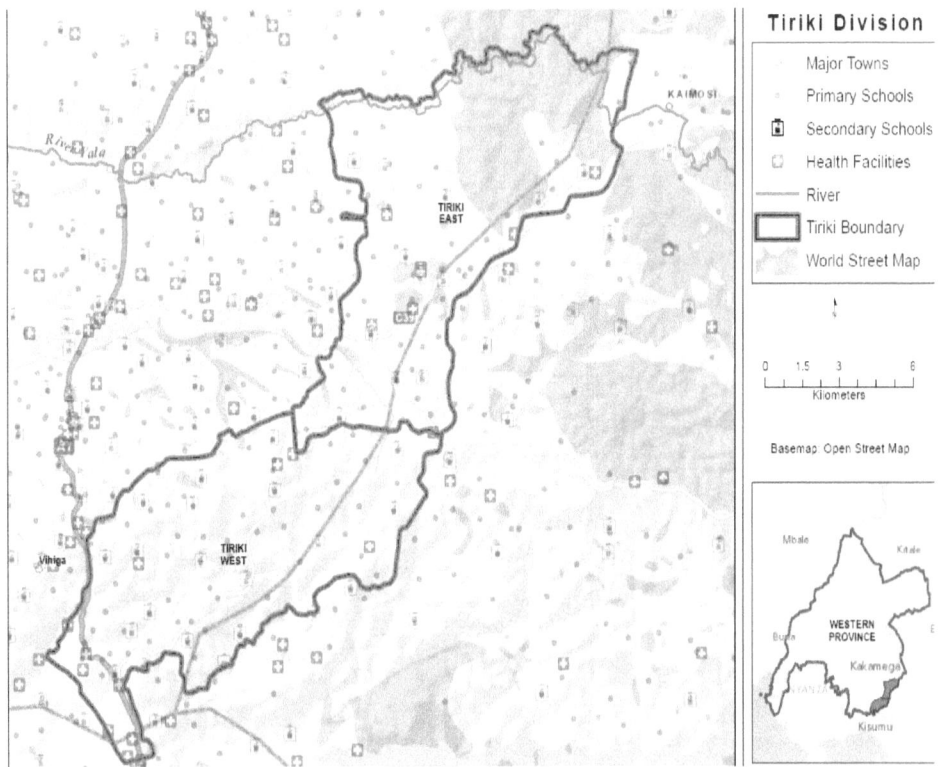

Figure 2.1
Tiriki Division
Source: Drawn by Samual Kimani

---

[2] Reading and writing had not yet been established among the Tiriki at the beginning of the 20th century. This date is basically an approximation, based on key events that can be remembered.

The Abasuba are one of the Bantu groups that migrated from Central Africa and settled in Tanzania. A further migration wave from the Suba in Tanzania settled on Rusinga Island in the vast Lake Victoria region. While the majority of Abasuba remained on Rusinga Island, there was a minor migration wave that crossed onto the mainland in the present day Nyanza and Western Provinces[3] of Kenya. Along the way, some members of the Abasuba settled among the Luo, Maragoli, Abanyole, Terik and Nandi communities. The spread of the Abasuba community is revealed in the following examples today: the late Tom Joseph Mboya's family in South Nyanza, the late Matayo Mwenesi's family in Maragoli, Festus Adoli's family at Lusengeli in Maragoli, and several Abasuba families in Tiriki, including Edgar Kadenyi of Alfayo Lundu's family at Shamakhokho, Daniel Choka's family at Mungavo, Reuben Yida's family at Senende, Saul Aluda's family at Mungavo, Mbaya's family at Senende, Mudaida's family at Senende, Khasievera's family at Mungavo, James Khabongo's family at Virembe, Maduvwe's family at Erusui, Tom Songole's family at Shivembe and Daniel Undusu's family at Goibei. In the 1970s, the Abasuba in Hamisi formed a welfare association but it died off.

Khadambi, Abraham Khayesi's grandfather, is thought to have been among the earlier immigrants from Tanzania, who settled along the flat lands at the present day Senende, between hills facing the Nandi escarpment. Being newcomers in a foreign land, the location provided good pasture for their cattle, fresh water from nearby rivers, a parcel of fertile land for farming and security from the Nandi morans. Khadambi had a son known as Lugondi and five daughters known as Musonye, Ang'u, Khajeha (two sisters with same name) and Muhavani.

Khadambi was a warrior and reached the rank of a captain in his community's military system. Khadambi was ambushed and killed by Kalenjin warriors near his home at Senende as he was returning home from a peace-making meeting with the Nandi community elders. The story in the family has it that Khadambi died, bleeding from cuts on his lips inflicted by the Nandi warriors. Generally, there was often fighting over cattle and land among the neighbouring Kalenjin, Tiriki and Luo communities. Among the Luo, there are legendary figures like Lwanda Magere who led their community in fighting against the Nandi. Incidentally, Abraham Khayesi named

---

[3] Since the passing of a new Constitution in 2010, Kenya has been politically organized into 47 counties instead of eight provinces and several districts (Laws of Kenya, 2010).

two of his sons, Jeremiah and Zakaria, after his grandfather. The story in the family has it that Zakaria had a bleeding wound on his lip that was not responding to treatment. However, after he was given the name Khadambi, the wound stopped bleeding and healed. Zakaria Khadambi still has a mark of the wound on his lips.

Lugondi, who was Khadambi's son, moved from Senende, crossed River Izava towards the East and settled at present day Erusui village, which is between present-day Virembe and Erusui, where he lived until his death in 1933. There are several Abasuba families in Erusui village. The explanation for this move as told in the family is that the specific incident involving the death of Khadambi indicated in the preceding paragraph, made Lugondi abandon Senende village to inhabit a new site at Erusui. The Abasuba, like many African communities, believed that once blood had been shed at a site, the affected people needed to shift to a new place to avoid a repeat of the act unless a cleansing ceremony was carried out.

Lugondi and his first wife, Khadolwa, had six children altogether: four sons and two daughters. The boys were Indeje (first born who died in childhood), Musikali (second born who also died in childhood), Khayesi (who survived childhood and died in 1973) and John Asalache (born in 1910, who also survived childhood and died in 1985). The two daughters were Vwamula and Khalagayi. When his first wife, Khadolwa, died in 1923, Lugondi remarried Lumanye (nicknamed and popularly known as Isumu[4]). This process of remarriage by Lugondi explains why Abraham Khayesi and John Asalache had two step-brothers (Elisha Muchera and William Jeptuya[5]) and three step-sisters (Ziripa Indiavana, Loise Khavayi and Agnes Khasandi Indama). Like his father Khadambi, Lugondi was also a warrior and a community leader. Khadolwa died in 1923, and Lugondi died in 1933 as has already been indicated.

---

[4] The word "Isumu" means poison. The story in the extended family has it that Lumanye was given this nickname because her children died at young age. The name was meant to express her sorrow. The cultural interpretation was that she had become like poison to her children and this is why they died, one by one. Secondly, it was believed in the traditional society that such a bad name would ward off the evil spirits that brought death and other problems to families.

[5] Jeptuya is a Kalenjin name. The story in the extended family is that either Khadambi's wife (Khadolwa) or mother was a Nandi, which was one of the Kalenjin ethno-linguistic groups.

Abraham Khayesi and his brothers inherited the ancestral parcels of land at Erusui, as the main property from their father. At a tender age, Abraham Khayesi was charged with the responsibility of taking care of his siblings. He took in his brother, John Asalache, to care for him and later also took care of his step-sisters and brothers. He also cared for Lumanye, his step-mother, until she died in the late 1950s, and he oversaw her burial.

The preceding chapters have discussed the family and community into which Abraham Khayesi was born and raised, and from which God chose him to spread the good news about Jesus Christ to his community and beyond.

CHAPTER THREE
Marriage

The Tiriki, like other African communities, have rites of passage such as circumcision for males, a rite that marks the transition from childhood to adulthood. Like all boys in the Tiriki community, Abraham Khayesi was circumcised in 1920 when he was young. He was of the Maina age set and held the title *chivuleti* or captain, having been the first to be circumcised in his age set on the day the event took place. Having undergone circumcision, Abraham Khayesi was, by cultural expectation, a man who had been initiated into the secrets of his community, and was ready to marry and participate fully in the life of his community.

At circumcision, the boys would be kept in a secluded hut known as *irumbi* for about six months. They would be taught about their history and prepared or hardened for adult life through learning crafts. During this long period of stay, the boys would visit their homes but not enter the houses. They would be served ready food, which they would eat in a banana grove. The boys would look after cattle but go back to *irumbi* at night. They participated in a traditional dance known as *vukhulu* and drank alcohol. One of the messages they were given was that there was one more major transitional stage they would face in life known as *mulo* or death. The Tiriki have kept this rite up to the present day, of course with some changes in the duration of stay by the boys in the secluded hut. The Tiriki who converted to Christianity, especially the Pentecostal form of Christianity, found some elements of the traditional circumcision to be incompatible with their faith and they made adjustments to it as explained in a later section.

Abraham Khayesi married his first wife, Maria Khanyanji, in August 1925. His notes show that he paid bride price worth two goats, three cows and 24 Kenyan shillings. The bride price was collected from Abraham Khayesi's home by Paul Andambi, a brother to Maria Khanyanji. Abraham Khayesi's notes show that Abednego Aronya was his witness regarding the payment of bride price. Maria was the daughter of Vutembeshe Andambi and Salome Madadi of Chetamilu village in present-day Bugina Sub-location in Busali West Location in Vihiga County. Her ethno-linguo group was Abalogoli. She belonged to Vashivembe clan. Maria Khanyanji was the only daughter of her parents and had two brothers: Paul Andambi and

Bendicto Ambwa. Abraham and Maria got 12 children, three of whom died in childhood. Maria died in October 1945.

> **Recollection**
>
> *Isaac Shadora recalls that Maria Khanyanji left behind a very young baby, Wilfas, who was still being breastfed. John Ingosi, who served as Church Secretary to Abraham Khayesi, remembers that some women from the village at times breastfed Wilfas. Isaac also recalls that a missionary by the name Fredrick Clark, who was based at Goibei Mission Station, brought a milk bottle for Wilfas which was used to keep the milk from Khayesi's cows to feed the young baby. Family members remember Maria Khanyanji as a loving and dedicated lady, who worked side by side with Abraham Khayesi in his pastoral work.*

Abraham Khayesi remarried in 1946 to Sabeti Shanyisa after the death of his first wife, Maria Khanyanji. According to notes in his book, he paid five cows and 210 Kenyan shillings as bride price for Sabeti Shanyisa. He first paid four cows and 210 Kenyan shillings in 1946. The fifth cow was paid on 16 September 1961. Sabeti Shanyisa and her family were living at Goibei. A widow or widower often faces the option to remarry or stay single. In the case of Abraham Khayesi, in addition to his own personal choice, there was also communal and church counsel for him to remarry, especially in view of the Church responsibilities he had and young orphans who needed care. The wedding of Abraham Khayesi and Sabeti Shanyisa was conducted by Fredrick Clark, a missionary based at Goibei Mission Station. Their bestman was Simeon Makhumbili and the best lady was Tabitha Khang'ahi. Their wedding registrar was Zakayo Imbukule.

Sabeti Shanyisa was born on 25 December 1924 in Bumbo village to Lazaro Muchwanda and Reba Aduvukha. She was dedicated to God as a baby in the Friends Church at Kaimosi by Daudi Lung'aho in 1925. She was the first born in a family of 14 children, comprising of six girls and eight boys. Her siblings were Rael Khasigani, Margaret Irago, Daniel Mutsi, Peris Maraga, Jonah Shavisa, Rhoda Khavagali, Selina M'mbone, Solomon Shavola and Rebecca Mukhusia. Her family migrated from Bumbo to Goibei and later migrated back to Bumbo (Figure 2.1). Sabeti belonged to Vavuluje clan. She started formal education in 1934 at Goibei Primary School. She completed class Sub B, equivalent to Standard three in modern Kenyan system of formal education. Her teachers were Daniel Undusu and Paul Jumba. One of Sabeti Shanyisa's classmates was Norah Khavosa Sangale. Sabeti Khayesi was baptized in water by Zakayo Munyasa in 1945. Her parents, Lazaro Muchwanda and Reba Aduvukha, died in 1962 and 1970, respectively. Sabeti Shanyisa was filled with the Holy Spirit, nursed and remained with this grace, including the gift of speaking in tongues, up to the time of her death in 2008.

Reba Aduvukha, mother of Sabeti Shanyisa.

Abraham Khayesi, Solomon Shavola (his brother in-law) and Sabeti Shanyisa, Nairobi, 1968, when Abraham khayesi visited his daughter Sarah who had been hospitalized in Kiambu.

Abraham Khayesi and Sabeti Shanyisa also had 12 children, eight boys and four girls. Three of their first children who were boys died in childhood and two died in adulthood. The names of the 18 children of Abraham Khayesi who survived childhood are shown in Table 3.1.

Table 3.1

Children of Abraham Khayesi who survived childhood

Name of Child	Name of Child
Jeremiah Khadambi	Zakaria Khadambi
Debla Khasoha	John Amayi
Mark Mugadia	Marie Khanyanji
Sarah Adolwa	Margaret Khashindu
Peris Lumedwa	Painito Ajanga
William Lugondi	Fridah Khasigani
Isaac Shadora	James Shisigani
Rabecca Khajeha	Meleckidzedeck Khayesi
Wilfas Vudembeshe	Abigail Mmbone

In addition to these 18 children, there are daughters-in law and sons-in law as well as grandchildren and great grand-children. Some of the sons-in-law and daughters-in-law have died. Details on names of daughters-in-law and sons-in-law as well as how the Khayesi family has faired on are provided in chapter nine.

The preceding information indicates that Abraham, Maria and Sabeti had a great social network and responsibility: 18 children, several sons-in law and daughters-in law, their own brothers and sisters, extended family members, relatives and members of the community. As it is the case in many families around the world, the Khayesi family is part of a community of relationships through marriage, friendship and relationships with other families, members of the community and institutions. The next chapters present the work of Abraham Khayesi as a Church pastor and a member of his local community.

CHAPTER FOUR
Conversion to Christianity

As it happened with many Africans who converted to Christianity, Abraham Khayesi initially followed the religious beliefs and practices of his community, the Tiriki. Mbiti (1961) pioneered writing on African traditional religious beliefs. Other writers, including literary scholars, have expanded on this work and highlighted key aspects of African beliefs to include belief in a supreme being, emphasis on consequences of one's actions, practice of religion in day-to-day life, sacrificing and performing religious rituals, a belief in *zamani*[6] and emphasis on communal belonging (Mbiti 1961, Shisanya 1996). While a number of these beliefs and practices still exist, they have been affected by interaction with other faiths and cultures such as Christianity, Islam, Hinduism, Westernization and Orientalization. Inculturation of African religious beliefs and practices is one of the long-standing issues examined by scholars of religion (Shisanya 1996, Wamue 2001). Khadambi Asalache (1967), who was a nephew of Abraham Khayesi, has provided a detailed description of love, war and intrigue in a traditional community in a novel known as *A Calabash of Life*.

Abraham Khayesi converted to Christianity, first briefly as a member of the Roman Catholic Church, from 1918 to 1926. The Roman Catholic Church station at Erusui was established as part of the spread of this denomination from Eregi, Mukumu and Kakamega. Some members of the Tiriki community did not fully embrace Catholicism by then and some joined the Friends Africa Mission Church also. The Tiriki traditional culture and related rituals were very strong. Changing from the community beliefs and rituals was treated as taboo to the community and the person who converted to another foreign faith was regarded as an outcast. Abraham Khayesi joined the likes of his agemates like Adanasi Mwirotsi, who later became a catechist in the Roman Catholic Church congregation at Erusui. After training in Roman Catholic Church catechism for a year, Khayesi was baptized and given the name Abraham. It must

---

[6] Zamani refers to the world of the living dead (Mbiti, 1961; Shisanya, 1996).

be remembered that Africans who converted to Christianity would take on or be given European names, which were then considered Christian names. This issue later became controversial among some African scholars and politicians who insisted that it is not a name that made one a Christian. They further argued that one could retain their African names and still be a Christian. There were indeed cases in which some Africans dropped their European Christian names in favour of their African names.

According to notes that Abraham Khayesi wrote, he moved from the Roman Catholic Church to the Friends Quaker Church in 1926. In these notes, Abraham Khayesi simply states, without giving details, that Tiriki people rejected or did not fully welcome Catholicism. The Friends Quaker Church had been established at Kaimosi in 1902 by three missionaries from the United States of America: Arthur Chilson, Willis Hotchkiss and Edgar Hole (Wafula 2001). Kaimosi became a key centre for the Friends Africa Mission. It developed educational, health, agricultural, industrial and theological institutions that provided services to the local community and other parts of Kenya. One of the industrial institute missionary leaders the local Tiriki community remembers, especially elderly people, was called Hoyt. They remember him for woodwork and also for putting up a maize grinding mill. From Kaimosi, the Friends Quaker Church reached other parts of Kenya and established mission centres and institutions in such places as Lirhanda, Kakamega, Lugulu, Vokoli, Kapsabet and Nairobi in Kenya, as well as neighbouring countries of Uganda and Tanzania.

Oral sources partly attribute Abraham Khayesi's change to the Friends Quaker Church to advice from his mother. The sources indicate that Khadolwa, Abraham Khayesi's mother, had converted to Christianity and fellowshipped in a Church; perhaps a Quaker or a Roman Catholic denomination. One of the stories in the family is that Abraham Khayesi often said that before his mother died, she told him to follow the religion or Church of the *vasungu* (whites), which at that time was the Friends Quaker Church that had come to Tiriki. "Learn how to read the Bible and pray to God so that you may see light in the future", Khadolwa is claimed to have said to her sons. Abraham Khayesi was a member of the Friends Quaker Church until 1932.

Sowing a seed of faith and hope

It must be remembered that in 1927[7], an important aspect of Pentecostal worship is reported to have occurred in the Friends Church at Kaimosi, namely, the outpouring of the Holy Spirit. John Ingosi, a former Church Secretary at Virembe PAG Church, recalls that the revival at Kaimosi started with preaching to Bible College students. The main speakers were Chilson and Ford. The eye witnesses have it that Mrs. Chilson spoke to the students about baptism in the Holy Spirit, which she herself had experienced while on holiday in the United States of America. It is reported that while she was speaking, the students received this baptism and started speaking in tongues. This experience at Kaimosi is identified as the beginning of a spiritual revival that spread in most of Western Kenya. Chilson and Ford returned to the United States of America in 1928, and were replaced by missionaries who were not familiar with the Pentecostal experience of speaking in tongues. This partly explains why the tongue-speaking members were excommunicated from worship in Quaker Friends Church congregations, with some being charged in a court of law. The Pentecostal experience was seen by the new missionaries and some of the old Christians as fanatical. John Ingosi further recalls that those who spoke in tongues would be restricted from attending Church for three months. John Ingosi reported that this group that had a different style of worship started meeting and fellowshipping secretly, paving the way to a Pentecostal group around Kaimosi. John Ingosi recalls that one day, while in fellowship, this group said it had a vision from God showing them that a white missionary would come from Kiboswa.

The oral sources indicate that Abraham Khayesi and others were physically beaten and excommunicated from the Friends Quaker Church because their members displayed a different style of worship that was not practised in their congregations. This style of worship included praying aloud and for many hours, speaking in a new or different language when praying (known as speaking in tongues),

---

[7] The 1927 revival at Kaimosi Friends Church Mission and its surrounding congregations in Tiriki and Maragoli was often and still is narrated by Pentecostals in this region. Samita (1992) shows that this revival partly led to the development of the African Church of the Holy Spirit. In addition, there is a group that joined the Pentecostal Missionaries that had just established a station at Nyang'ori, near Kisumu (Kavaya 2003). While 1927 may not be the exact year when Abraham Khayesi and others left the Friends Quaker Church, the key point is that the revival that started this year saw the emergence of a Pentecostal group that grew and established a separate fellowship, in partnership with another Pentecostal group of Whites, in the years that followed.

openly repenting or confessing sins, and prophesying. It was during one such beating that Abraham Khayesi is reported to have had one or two of his ribs broken. Speaking in tongues was not a typical way of worship in the Friends Quaker Church. Thus, while in the Friends Quaker Church, Abraham Khayesi had a deeper spiritual experience; an experience that virtually many or all Pentecostal preachers and the clergy would indicate they had had, leading to an acute sense of the need to preach repentance to the world.

One of the stories I had heard is that this tongue-speaking group was described as speaking the language of the Nyang'ori people (see Box 1.1). The deeper conversion while in Friends Quaker Church marked an important turning point in the life of Abraham Khayesi and several others as this experience led him into Pentecostalism, which was characterized by a deep sense of the need to change from sin and live a life pleasing to God in order to go to heaven. In addition, Pentecostals were known for speaking in tongues, vigorous worship, singing, dancing and emphasis on an experiential encounter with God through Jesus Christ. These are distinctive features of Pentecostals around the world. The Pentecostal experience described here resembles more or less the same experience that has been reported in such places as Azusa Street (McGee 2005). Abraham Khayesi's notes show that he left the Friends Quakers Church in August 1932 and joined a Pentecostal fellowship. Abraham Khayesi was baptized in water in 1933.

Box 4.1

PAOC and PAG

The reference to Nyang'ori people is not necessarily to the people who lived around Nyang'ori but rather to the Pentecostal missionaries who had recently established a base at Nyang'ori, near Kisumu. PAOC began its work in Kenya in 1918, with a mission station at Nyang'ori, near Kisumu (PAOC archives, 26 December 2012, Manana 2000). It should also be noted that there were other Christian Missions that were then either recently established or being established in Western Kenya at more or less the same time as the Friends Quaker Church, PAOC/PAG and the Roman Catholic Church. The key ones were Salvation Army, Church of God (with Headquarters at Kima in Bunyore) and Church Missionary Society/Anglican Church. I hope to prepare a comprehensive book on the history of PAOC and PAG in East Africa and Kenya.

The spirit filled-tongue-speaking group left the Friends Quaker Church and joined or established new Pentecostal denominations. One group spread toward Idakho, led by Mavuru and formed the African Church of the Holy Spirit Church. The history of this group, especially its beliefs and practices related to the Holy Spirit, has been studied and documented in detail by Samita (1992). The other group, led by Zakayo Munyasa, Abraham Khayesi, Saul Aluda, Saul Amuhaya, Bulemi and others, sought nurturing and collaboration with Otto Keller's PAOC mission at Nyang'ori. The oral sources indicated that this group was introduced to Otto Keller by Zakaria Oyiengo and Zakayo Shivuli, who was a cook at Keller's house. Oyiengo and Shivuli were brothers. John Ingosi recalls 1933 to be the year this group met Otto Keller and he says they were led by Matia Elanogwa. Incidentally, there was also another group of Pentecostals that had formed or was forming in Maragoli. Keller eventually accepted this Pentecostal group and together, they formed a fellowship known as *Vabende* (pentecostals), which laid the foundation for the birth of the PAG Church in Kenya. The group is reported to have stayed for two nights at Nyang'ori centre, before returning back to the village. They were assured of future continuity with a denomination that believed in speaking in different tongues as the Holy Spirit guided them.

There may be specific details that different individuals who have participated in the Pentecostal experience will emphasize, but what emerges from the various narratives is as follows:

- Abraham Khayesi was among the group of worshippers who had a Pentecostal experience while fellowshipping in Friends Quaker Church;
- The baptism in the Holy Spirit is traced to a 1927 meeting at Kaimosi, in which the main speakers were Chilson and Ford;
- The tongue-speaking group was not readily accommodated in Friends Quaker Church, following the departure of Chilson and Ford. The group was excommunicated from many Friends Quaker Church congregations in Tiriki, Maragoli and other parts of Western Kenya. The group often reported that its members were physically beaten and in some incidents charged in a court of law because of its style of behaviour which was thought to be fanatical;
- The tongue-speaking group (the Pentecostals) started worshipping secretly on their own;

- This Pentecostal group got to know about the presence of Otto Keller, a white Pentecostal missionary, who had established a mission station at Nyang'ori;
- In 1933, the tongue-speaking, Pentecostal group that had left Friends Quaker Church held a meeting with Otto Keller, leading to consensus to work or fellowship together, which led to further expansion of PAOC;
- Among the local pentecostals who emerged as leaders of *Vabende* were Matia Elanogwa, Zakayo Munyasa and Abraham Khayesi. These local leaders established and led congregations in such places as Madira, Tsimbalo, Mahanda, Museywa, Shiru, Mungavo, Virembe, Simbi and Goibei.

Abraham Khayesi and a group of his fellow Pentecostals contributed to the establishment of the first PAOC congregation in Tiriki at Mungavo in 1933. Abraham Khayesi's records show the following as among the founding members of the PAOC congregation at Mungavo: Zakayo Munyasa, Thomasi Khigani, Musa Khazalwa, Stephano Shimejera, Yosto Jirongo, Daniel Choka, Sarah Mukhunji, Robai Namatsi, Siriya Khamoji, Joseph Alulu, Abraham Khayesi, Margaret Khisavalu, Rabecca Ashiundu, Saul Aluda, David Kituda, Jacob Malova, Paul Mbiri, Esteri Isilinji, Dina Khavugwi, Lenah Indongole, Priscila Shijedi, Elisha Mujera, Samuel Anyambu and Robai Khadovonje. The second PAOC congregation in Tiriki was at Virembe in 1934, with some members moving from Mungavo to establish this new congregation. Zakayo Munyasa was a pastor at Virembe Assembly from 1934 to 1937. Abraham Khayesi became the second pastor of Virembe PAOC Assembly from 1938 to 1967. One of the early converts to Pentecostalism recalled that Virembe derived its name from a Luhya sacred tree called *Murembe*. The site had a large collection of *mirembe* trees. It was an open place (*luhya*) that belonged to the community and would be used for meetings, dances and other general uses. The setting up of a church at this site transformed the traditional heritage into a Christian centre. The local community used *Murembe* for traditional cleansing, cultural oathing and cure of mumps *(Tsindendeyi)*. It was neither used for firewood nor as a shade by people who would have wanted to sit under it.

The Mungavo Pentecostal group, which was led by Zakayo Munyasa and comprised of Saul Aluda, Tomasi Khiganili, Musa Khazalwa, Paul Mbiri, Rabeka Ashiundu Aluda, Reba Mbiri, among others, continued to grow. The Virembe Pentecostal group including

Benjamin Sangale, Yosto Jirongo, Musa Natse, Saul Amuhaya, Paulo Shivachi, Abednego Aronya, Musa Shihumbu, Samuel Anyambu, Reuben Mbali, Paulo Jirongo, Rabeka Vudakha, Gladys Vusisa and Selina Lulia, among others, also continued to grow. Abraham Khayesi pioneered and also helped in the establishment of several other Pentecostal congregations in Tiriki, as well as other parts of Western Kenya and Uganda. As already stated, there were also several leaders who pioneered or contributed to the establishment of Pentecostal congregations or fellowships in several places such as Madira, Mbale, Shiru, Museywa, Givogi and Goibei. The provincial administration is also reported to have been accommodative and supportive of the Pentecostal group and did not try to stop it from operating.

One of the intriguing incidents told is that Abraham Khayesi witnessed to his friend known as Stephano Shamajere from Idakho. Upon conversion, Stephano experienced some unacceptance or hostility from some members of the Friends Quaker Church. He relocated with his family to live on the Church compound at Virembe in Tiriki. He lived there for a number of years. In fact, while living at Virembe[8], Stephano's wife passed on and he remarried. With the help of missionaries from Nyang'ori, Abraham Khayesi helped to plant or start a Church in Stephano's local area, at Virembe in Idakho. Stephano moved back to his local home area and spearheaded the planting of PAOC congregations in Idakho and Isukha. Stephano remained in contact with Abraham Khayesi and Nyang'ori Pentecostal Mission Headquarters.

Many of the founding members who were also pioneer leaders and lay people have since died. A few of the local leaders grew to national and international stature. For example, Isaac Khaguli moved from being a local pastor to a national and international evangelist, working under PAOC/PAG (K). He later founded a fellowship or an evangelistic group known as Pentecostal Evangelistic Team, which still exists today.

The traditional environment in Tiriki continued to be hostile to those who had converted to Christianity, particularly those who had cut links with the traditional circumcision rites and other rituals such as traditional African religious worship. Instead of circumcising

---

[8] This name may be confusing as to what place it is referring to but it needs to be noted that different places often share the same name. We have made an effort to distinguish this issue as much as possible.

boys according to the traditional rituals, the Christian converts organized their own ceremonies in which they taught the boys about the Bible. Zakayo Munyasa, Abraham Khayesi, Saul Aluda and other Christians teamed up and initiated a circumcision for Tiriki boys based on Christian values. The traditional Tiriki circumcision was headed by Sakwa (at that particular time). His wife, Damara, who had converted to Christianity, secretly passed her son to the Christian circumcision group, which became an important breakthrough to transforming Tiriki traditions and circumcision rites.

During the circumcision period, those who still practised the original traditional rite would sing abusive and character-assassinating songs towards the Christian converts. A number of African writers such as Ngugi wa Thiong'o (1965), Chinua Achebe (1958) and Okot p'Bitek (1966) have written extensively about the conflict between the local culture and Christianity on such issues as circumcision, marriage and worshipping the supreme being of the African communities versus the God of Christianity. It was not different in Tiriki from the early days of Christian converts up to a few years ago. The Christian converts held to their faith, committing themselves not to go back to the traditional circumcision; a number of whose practices, they felt were not in harmony with their newly found faith.

There were also groups that branched from PAOC. For example, in 1942, Zakayo Kivuli separated from PAOC and founded the African Israel Nineveh Church (AINC), with a good understanding between Zakayo Kivuli and PAOC Mission at Nyang'ori. AINC pastors have for a long period of time trained at Pentecostal Bible College at Nyang'ori until recently when AINC started its own Bible school. AINC fully participated in the vigil service by PAOC missionaries, local pastors and church members to mourn and bury Otto Keller in 1942 at the Nyang'ori mission compound. One of the stories in AINC is that Pentecostal missionaries at Nyang'ori, Goibei, Nairobi and Kisumu buy their Christmas turkeys from AINC headquarters. Another encouraging ecumenical approach is that trained pastors from PAG (K), AINC and African Divine Church can freely serve or pray for members of each group without it raising a big issue. There are also groups that branched off such as Roho People or Musalaba People (1934), Pentecostal Fellowship (1936), African Divine Church (1948), PAG Nyanza (1939), Holiness Church (1972) and Pentecostal Evangelism Team (1976). These fellowships are not the core subject

Sowing a seed of faith and hope

matter of this book. We hope to cover them in another book that will examine the history of PAOC/PAG[9] in Kenya and East Africa.

---

[9] PAG (K) came into existence in 1964 as a Kenyan pentecostal fellowship. It has maintained a working relationship with PAOC.

CHAPTER FIVE
Education

Basic formal education

Abraham Khayesi received the education of his Tiriki community. As it happened in many African communities, the Christian missionaries introduced formal education. The Friends Quaker Church missionaries at Kaimosi did the same. An oral source indicated that Abraham Khayesi was among the first group of Tiriki boys, probably aged 12-15 years, whom the Quaker Friends Church missionaries taught basic reading skills using cloth materials locally known as *tsinanga*. He is reported to have attended classes A, B, C and D for basic oral reading and writing lessons. *Tsinanga* was a large piece of cloth with inscribed letters for oral reading.

Theological training and ordination

Zakayo Munyasa, Abraham Khayesi, Saul Aluda and several others became leaders or pastors without formal theological training. PAOC started the Pentecostal Bible Institute at Goibei Mission in 1941 under the leadership of a missionary known as Mark Bright. Abraham Khayesi was among the first trainees in 1941. His notes indicate that he felt the call of God to go to the Bible School at Goibei. The first class had five students: Matia Elanogwa, Joel Chamwada, Abraham Khayesi, Isaya Khayeli and Daudi Chole. They were taught theology, reading, handwriting and arithmetic. Their tutors were Fredrick Clark and his wife. Daniel Undusu, who was a trained primary school teacher and later became a pastor, was the interpreter from English to Luhya. Abraham Khayesi and his fellow classmates trained for two years and graduated as pastors. These mature students were trained as the local leaders to take further the spread of the gospel in Kenya and beyond. On completion of the training, these pioneer students continued with pastoral work and were posted to local areas and also undertook responsibilities beyond their immediate congregations in places like Boma, Virembe, Goibei, Itegero, Tsimbalu, Chemovo, Madira, Kapsengere, Gee, Kasiani, Shiru, Ivola, Museywa, Kisii, Bugisu, Nairobi, Gimaragwa, Kamarenga, Ivonda, Busia, Bunyore, Givogi, Simbi, Idakho, Mungavo and Gitagwa. Abraham Khayesi's notes show that in 1942, while at Goibei mission, he bought a cow from Fredrick Clark at a price of 90 Kenyan shillings. He contributed 50 Kenyan shillings and Matayo Atsianji contributed 40 Kenyan shillings. His notes provide intriguing details: the cow had a black body and a white face; witnesses to the transaction are given as Daniel Undusu, Isaya Khayeri, Saulo Maleya, Elikana Madekhale, Joel Shamwada, Zakaria Oyengo, Zakayo Mbukhule, Saulo Aluda, Daudi Choka, Charles Muga, Liajimu Nyamboge and Zakayo Lilisandula; the date of the transaction is provided as 25 June 1942, and the mechanism of paying Matayo Atsianji is specified (he was given a female calf by Abraham Khayesi after the cow had given birth). This example of buying a cow shows how these mature pastor trainees straddled family responsibilities and Church work. It also reveals how they were practically applying some of the lessons they were learning, such as keeping records of key activities. The group effort in being witnesses or arrangements for repayment provides an interesting lesson in collective leadership, accountability, friendship and strategy.

In 1948, the Bible School was transferred from Goibei to Nyang'ori and was called Bethel Bible College and later changed to Pentecostal Bible College in 1949. Nyang'ori Mission Station also hosted primary, inter-mediate and secondary schools, a printing press and a teacher training college, which was later phased-out. Goibei, which was for a long period of time under the leadership of Iris Scheel, continued to run the following programmes: Christ Ambassadors, a youth camp for all Churches in Kenya, a boarding school for girls known as Goibei Girls High School, Christian Religious Education Awareness of Teachers and training of local missionaries for unreached areas (Manana 2012). Currently, Gobei has a private Primary Teachers' College, a sanctuary, a secondary boarding school for girls, and a mixed primary school.

The theological training enabled Abraham Khayesi not only to learn about the Bible but also to learn how to read and write for himself, which was beneficial to both the Church and his family. He was able to keep good records for his family and the Church, some of which are still available and were helpful in preparing this book (see Box 5.1). One of the sources I have used is a notebook in which Abraham Khayesi has kept details of his children, key family events, transactions and even written out copies of letters sent and received. John Amayi, one of Abraham Khayesi's sons, was the main scribe to Abraham Khayesi in the preparation of the notes which were useful in detailing the life story of Abraham Khayesi. This note book was helpful in identifying issues that needed to be probed further from people interviewed during data collection. Abraham was also

Sowing a seed of faith and hope

able to write letters to his children who were in boarding schools or were working in other places like Mombasa, as well as friends, administrators and fellow pastors. Abraham Khayesi had a cupboard in his house in which he kept his family and Church records. On several occasions, Sabeti Khayesi would comically laugh after supper and prayers, telling her children:

"Do you know why your father (Abraham) went to school at an older age? His brother, Asalache, went to work for the whites in Nairobi. Asalache wrote to him a letter. The only person who could read and write letters in this village was the catholic catechist. Abraham took the letter to him. He asked your father to go cutting thatching sticks from nearby bushes per every sentence he read for Abraham. Since this local catechist was his age-mate, Abraham disliked the idea and decided to learn how to read and write at an older age. By the way, he succeeded and became an ordained pastor achieving the highest title in PAG known as reverend. Take your books now and read seriously".

Box 5.1

Practice of record keeping by Abraham Khayesi

Abraham Khayesi had a good practice of record keeping. He had notebooks in which he wrote by himself and with the help of scribes key events and transactions in his life. The page below shows details he wrote on the construction of his brick house: costs of construction materials and labour as well as names of workers.

After the theological training, Abraham Khayesi continued to work as a pastor at Virembe PAOC/PAG Church, where he served up to 1967. Family and Church members remember that Abraham Khayesi always prepared and planned his sermons. He studied the Bible and made notes during the week as he also attended to family, community and Church responsibilities.

It took five years after training during which one was observed, guided and given further instructions before ordination. Kavaya (2003) reports that in 1948, during the first PAG General Conference, Roy Upton, the General Superintendent of PAOC in Kenya for the period 1942-1948, conducted the first PAG ordination service at Nyang'ori. The first 13 local pastors who were ordained and given the title reverend[10] were: Matia Elanogwa, Daudi Chole, Joel Chamwada, Isaya Khayeli, Abraham Khayesi, Saul Aluda, Zakayo Imbukule, Eliakim Nyambu, Saulo Maleya, Samson Asena, Zakaria Oyengo, James Goligo and Charles Omuga.

---

[10] The position of a reverend in Pentecostal Assemblies of God (Kenya) is bestowed on pastors who have been observed and found committed, faithful and living in accordance with Biblical principles. A reverend performs several duties: baby dedication, serving Holy Communion, conducting water baptism, preaching, counselling Church members, conducting burial services and spreading the gospel. He or she is expected to be a role model and an ambassador of Jesus Christ in all aspects of life.

CHAPTER SIX

Beyond officially defined boundaries

A small beginning

The early communicants at Virembe PAOC were fewer in number. Right from the beginning, a number of the local community members who had not converted to Christianity became hostile to the Christian faith. They looked at Pentecostalism as a spoiler of Tiriki culture and traditions, especially the circumcision of boys. As a result of this opposition, the Christian church members were persecuted, including physical beating and burning of their grass-thatched houses. One of the approaches used by the Virembe Church to evangelize the local community was through door-to-door witnessing. A group of Church members moved from one home to another, sharing the gospel, and praying for those who converted to Christianity.

Abraham Khayesi and Sabeti Shanyisa outside their house at Erusui village before setting off to Church (Copyright: Khadambi Khayesi)

Virembe Pentecostal Assemblies of God grows into a key operational base

For over 30 years, Abraham Khayesi's Christian work and service was based at Virembe PAOC/PAG Church. PAG has a participatory and congregational approach to leadership. In addition to the overall pastors, there are other leaders for youth, women, Sunday school and general administration. Different professionals like deacons, women directors and church secretaries worked under the leadership of Abraham Khayesi at Virembe church. For instance, Yosto Jirongo, Joshua Ayodi, Paul Jirongo, Reuben Mbali and Samuel Anyambu worked as deacons. Ester Lwova Smith (1948-1953) and Jerita Imbusi (1955-1967) worked as women directors. Abedinego Aronya, Simioni Makhumbili, Joseph Masere and John Ingosi worked as church secretaries.

In addition to the local Church leaders, Abraham Khayesi worked with and also under several PAOC/PAG missionaries and overall leaders. The General Superintendents he worked under were Otto Keller (1927-1942), Roy Upton (1944-1948), R. Morrison (1948-1965), Matia Elanogwa (1965-1969) and Charles Gungu (1969-1975).

Abraham Khayesi (fifth from right in standing row) with PAOC and PAG (K) leaders in the 1960s

Virembe Pentecostal Assemblies of God Church progressively became a key congregation in the spread of the gospel not only in Tiriki but also the rest of the then Kakamega District and Western Kenya. The importance of Virembe PAG as a centre in the Pentecostal work is noted in several key areas.

The first reason for the importance of Virembe Pentecostal Assemblies is that several Christian conventions (*vibenzeni*) and outreach meetings were held at this site. The conventions lasted for seven or eight days. John Ingosi remembers that during these conventions, about 12 bulls were slaughtered to feed the large number of participants. Eye witnesses remember that Iris Scheel, who headed the Christ Ambassadors (CA) programme, provided and showed Christian films in the evenings during these conventions. A memorable incident talked about at one of these conventions is that there was a missionary who preached for about 40 minutes and then the congregation knelt on their knees and started praying at about 12:30 pm and went on praying until after 6:00 pm. The missionary preacher got out through a window while Abraham Khayesi and the deacons remained to take care of the praying congregation. A number of missionaries such as John Lyn and Heinz Battermann conducted meetings at this site. One of the missionary meetings that some of the older members remember was by Bengo from South Africa, who held a service for a week in which people were saved, restored and healed. Virembe congregation also reached the local community with the gospel. By evangelizing to the local community and providing messages of hope in God, the Virembe congregation helped to counter unproductive local traditions of witchcraft leaders who were well known in the local community. Those who embraced Christianity felt empowered to ignore and overcome belief and practices of witchcraft.

> **Recollection**
>
> *"While I lived at Goibei and Kakamega, I worked very closely with your father and I learned to respect him and his wisdom and love for the Lord" (John Lynn, 24 January 2003, E-mail to Meleckidzedeck Khayesi).*

The second reason is that Virembe was a focal point for the annual water baptism which was held for the first time at a swampy place in the village of Shirongo along River Izava. Older members remember how missionaries like Otto Keller, assisted by Abraham Khayesi and others, would come to conduct the baptism. Water baptism preparatory classes lasted for one year. The final intense preparations involved the candidates withdrawing from their homes and staying at the Church for four days, holding prayers, repenting of any sins and seeking for baptism in the Holy Spirit. This intense preparation culminated in water baptism, with many Christians singing and welcoming the new converts. The venue of the water baptism service was later moved down the river to Lwandoni bridge due to availability of more space; it has remained there up to date.

The third reason is that Virembe was a burial site for Christians who lived in this area and even beyond. John Ingosi remembers that Abraham Khayesi facilitated the establishment of a burial site at this

Water baptism by a group of PAG (K) congregations in December 2016

Church. Among the notable graves located on the church compound is that of the mother of the late Musa Amalemba, the first Legislative Council member from Western Kenya, who hailed from Shinyalu area, which is a distance of about 40 kilometres away.

The fourth reason is that a number of PAG assemblies started off as either outposts of Virembe or their leaders were nurtured in this congregation or Abraham Khayesi contributed to their establishment. The model in operation then was the creation of congregational outposts, as the faith and believers spread further and further. This meant that as the number of believers living further away from a main congregation increased, a small outpost would be started. They would hold fellowships in these outposts but come together for a major fellowship then known locally as *isalasini* (literally meaning thirty), which was held on the last Sunday of the month. From Virembe, a number of outposts and later major congregations grew. Among the congregations that Abraham, Maria and Sabeti Khayesi assisted with establishing, as well as putting up buildings in Tiriki included Bumira, Shamalago, Bumbo, Ivoida, Wasenje, Jevusasuli, Shirongo, Idulu, Jemulongoji, Chepkwoni, Shiru, Lulali, Vuronya, Cheptembuli and Erusui.

The fifth reason is that Virembe, like other PAG congregations, started an elementary primary school. In 1940, a missionary known as Clark granted permission to Zakayo Munyasa and Abraham Khayesi to start a junior primary school (Standard 1-4) at Virembe. This development was important in enabling children whose parents belonged to PAG to have access to basic education, and then proceed to upper primary and later to secondary education at Goibei Girls High School in the case of girls and Nyang'ori Secondary School in the case of boys. There was also a teacher training college at the Pentecostal Assemblies of God Mission Station at Nyang'ori. Among the young people who went through Virembe School and moved to Nyang'ori upper primary are Elikana Sawe and Eliud Shamagovi. These young people later played important roles as teachers, Church secretaries and role models in the society. It must be remembered that at that time, admission to schools was based on denomination. The Friends African Mission and Roman Catholic Churches also had their own primary and secondary schools.

In all the areas summarized above, Abraham Khayesi, Maria Khanyanji and Sabeti Shanyisa worked closely and in partnership with other pastors, missionaries and members of Virembe Pentecostal Assemblies of God congregation in spreading the Gospel of God. A number of the respondents interviewed during data collection mentioned several pastors and people that Abraham Khayesi, Maria Khanyanji and Sabeti Shanyisa worked with in spreading the Gospel, with many of them becoming their close friends. These included: Zakayo Munyasa, Saul Aluda, Zakaria Oyengo, Zakayo Mbukule, Daudi Vulemi, Isaya Khayeri, Shem Irangi, Zakaria Yengo, Joshua Ayodi, Mark Khejeri, Musa Natse, John Ingosi, Benjamin Sangale, Joel Gitiva, among others.

> Mutembe
>
> Kay 30.5.40
>
> Ndio sisi Mukutano Ka Bitembe pamoja nawao wamukutano Zakayo. Munyasa na Abrahamu kwa wote wamekubali Junior school Utakuwa Inya tunakata pamoja na Bwana Clarke.
>
> J. Clarke

In addition to giving pastoral services to the congregation and attending to specific activities such as counselling, praying for the sick, conducting wedding ceremonies, dedicating babies, conducting water baptism services and funeral services, Abraham Khayesi performed other roles and held various responsibilities such as treasurer and vice chairman in the local PAG administration as well as participating in deliberations, meetings and committees with other national leaders. It is important to note that a pastor's wife, as was the case with Maria Khanyanji and Sabeti Shanyisa, does not just complement or support the husband's work but also has distinctive roles and strictly speaking, is a pastor in her own right (Box 6.1). Though PAG (K) recognizes this distinctive role, it has rarely ordained wives of pastors as pastors in their own right.

Box 6.1

Sabeti Khayesi: multiple roles of a pastor's wife

While working closely with Abraham Khayesi, Sabeti Shanyisa had distinct roles she played in Church ministry and society. These roles included:

a. Leading women's ministry at the assembly and local levels;
b. Teaching Sunday school under the overall leadership of Iris Scheel. On a Sunday morning, Sabeti would collect virtually all the youth in the village, including her own children, and accompany them along the road to Virembe church for Sunday school lessons. She conducted the lesson involving the participation of both girls and boys in reading the Bible, reciting verses, singing, offertory, drama and chorals. Majority of her Sunday school pupils went on to become Sunday school teachers and leaders in various church departments. Her favourite song for the youth ministry was *Vanyerere Vosi* ("Faith is the Victory").

c. Conducting Christmas carols at the assembly level. During Sabeti's burial, the Church members honoured her for this role by singing a Christmas carol, "*Yesu yivulwa mu Bethelehemu*" and reciting a scripture (Mathew 2: 1-5) about the birth of Jesus Christ at her graveside;
d. Hosting several visiting pastors and Bible college students at her house;
e. Serving as a member of Church committees and boards;
f. Serving as a counsellor in the Church and local community;
g. Praying for the Church and local community members;
h. Holding prayers and fellowships in her house, especially for women. A number of my older siblings remember seeing Sabeti Shanyisa, Robai Khadovonje and other ladies leading or holding fellowships on Wednesday in her house. They discussed and prayed with a number of young ladies on issues related to marriage and life. Among the young ladies then who often talked about the benefits of these meetings were Rabeka Benderi, Zipporah Masere, Rodah Ingosi, Safina Asalache and Zipporah Jeptuya. These meetings also saw ladies in the community being led in repentance and conversion to Christianity; and
i. Sharing the gospel and material possessions with those in need.

Recollection

The children of Abraham Khayesi remember that their parents' home was open to many Christian and social activities. It looked like a mini-mission station. Below is a summary of some of the activities that the children remember taking place in their home:

a. A "Tukutendereza" group from Uganda visited and stayed with their parents in the early 1960s. Abraham Khayesi often sang this song, "Tukutendereza Yesu", in Luganda. He taught it to members of his congregation and it was a top hit during services.
b. Several national and local PAG leaders and pastors like Matthias Elanogwa, Charles Gungu and Stephano Shamajere frequently visited their parents to discuss PAG programmes and plan for Church activities.
c. A number of missionaries from abroad, for example, John Lynn and Clark, visited for consultation on outreaches to

Western Kenya and Uganda, or stayed in the home. For example, the Battermanns put up a tent in Abraham Khayesi's home compound in 1960 while preaching at Virembe PAG congregation for a week. Zakaria Khadambi remembers taking milk to the Battermanns at the tent and also riding in the backseat of their Volkswagen to services at Virembe. Zakaria Khadambi further recalls picking up Christian tracts on Sunday mornings that would be dropped at the gate to the home from Iris Scheel's vehicle by Mark Kidula and his wife, Emmy, who would be evangelizing to the youth as they passed by.

d. A student from the Pentecostal Bible College at Nyang'ori by the name David Omalla and his friend stayed in their parents' home in the 1960s while serving as interns at Virembe PAG Church, where Abraham Khayesi was a pastor. Interestingly, the son of Abraham Khayesi known as Meleckidzedeck Khayesi married the daughter of David Omalla known as Jane Nyakecho several years later in 1994.

e. Many Christians visited their parents for discussion and counselling on such issues as water and Holy Spirit baptism, marriage and general Christian living.

f. Their parents welcomed and accommodated young people, mostly girls, who had been rejected by their families because of converting to Christianity. An example mostly remembered is that of Selina Jirongo, whose wedding was conducted from the home of Abraham Khayesi because she had converted to Christianity and her family was hostile to her because of her new faith.

g. Their parents welcomed and offered accommodation to many strangers, lost and found children as well as travellers from far places who could not afford walking for long distances since the means of transport during those days was poor.

As I have listened to stories and examined records, I have come to learn that my father, Abraham Khayesi, served God beyond his officially designated congregation and community. It is apparent that he turned his officially designated congregation into a base to spread the gospel in collaboration with others. Beyond Tiriki, he was involved in spreading the gospel and founding congregations in Eldoret, Kakamega, Kabras, Busia, Isukha and Idakho. He was the local chairman of PAG in Kakamega, Kabras, Busia and Idakho.

Sowing a seed of faith and hope

One of the stories I came across is that Abraham Khayesi, Musa Natse, Zakayo Imbukule and Daudi Vulemi went to Uganda in the 1940s-1960s to spread the gospel among the Bagisu, Baganda and Teso. Notes in one of Abraham Khayesi's notebook show that he started preaching among the Abagisu in Uganda in 1942-1943.

> **Recollection**
>
> *Some of the things that Zakaria Khadambi, one of Abraham Khayesi's sons, remembers are the white nytil Jinja shirts, packed pork, furniture, new clothes and metal plates that our father used to bring for his family from Uganda. Mary Khanyanji, one of Abraham Khayesi's daughters, remembers that on his return from such missionary journeys, they would know he was coming from his humming, whistling or softly singing as he walked towards the house from the gate. He would then gather together those who were present for prayer. In the evening, he shared some information from his mission work, sang and taught his family some of the Christian songs he had learnt in the places he had visited. Indeed, older siblings remember that Abraham Khayesi had competence in singing and learning other languages such as Kalenjin, Kigusii and Luganda.*

Nurturing children

Abraham Khayesi, Maria Khanyanji and Sabeti Shanyisa did not only serve the Church and the community but also made an effort to nurture their children to be responsible and God-fearing. They always gathered their family around a table in the evening for prayer, scripture reading and teaching. The children often remind each other how their father would not hesitate to give them two or a few more strong canes using his leather belt or a stick if they made serious mistakes. They often got amused that their father would not only cane them but also explain the reason for the discipline and read or mention the relevant scripture to the offending child. He went further to ask the offender to repent for the mistake made, clearly terming it a sin. My older siblings muse that one caning experience with our father was enough and no one dared to repeat the mistake. Isaac Shadora remembers that Sabeti Shanyisa played a key role in helping Abraham Khayesi to discipline and nurture a fairly large number of children that he had. Isaac Shadora recalls that on some occasions where a few children would be overtly defiant and Abraham Khayesi would appear overwhelmed, Sabeti Shanyisa stepped in and brought things to order. Abraham Khayesi, Maria Khanyanji and Sabeti Shanyisa taught all their children to learn to ask for forgiveness or apologize for any wrong thing they did. This approach to discipline was generally used by the church deacons and Christians in their respective homes as a method of instilling discipline in the youth.

Our parents would not unrealistically cover their children's wrongs. However, they would take practical steps when there was a need for them to defend their children from unwarranted and unjustified harassment. A story is told of how Sabeti Khayesi stood up to a teacher who was unjustifiably punishing her step-son, Wilfas Vudembeshe. The story goes that this teacher would punish Wilfas for no apparent reason. When it continued for a while, Sabeti Khayesi went to the school and demanded to know why this unjustified and continued punishment was going on. It was discovered that the teacher had no good reason for punishing Wilfas other than wanting the boy to salute him every time he passed. The teacher later left the school and went to teach in a town school for several years.

Abraham Khayesi, Maria Khanyanji and Sabeti Shanyisa emphasized hard work and taking initiative to the extent that they literally applied Paul's principle of "no work, no food" (2 Thessalonians 3:10) to their children who had failed to perform daily chores such as fetching water, preparing food, cleaning the compound, looking after cattle and working on the farm. They also taught their children the importance of showing respect to other people, whether young or old. The children remember not only the teachings they received from their parents but also seeing them practise what they preached. Our parents would apologize even to their own children. One of the things we noticed in letters written by Sabeti Khayesi to her children and even during face-to-face discussion was that she would always ask for forgiveness for any wrong word she might have written in the letter or uttered during a discussion. As life experience has shown, teaching or educating a child and practising it are two different things. The truth of the matter is that while a number of the children of Abraham Khayesi tried to follow their parents' teaching, a few also rebelled as they grew older and did the opposite. What is interesting is that even those who rebelled tend to come back to the way their parents taught them as they (children) grew older.

Our parents had favourite hymns, choruses and scriptures. They would often sing Christian hymns and praises as they went about their day-to-day activities, which included milking cows, pruning coffee, ploughing the farm, preparing meals and other home chores.

Abraham Khayesi's children and family would always know when their baba would be returning home as there would be a preceding song and a chorus, on many occasions being whistled. The most favourite songs and praises of our parents were: *Yesu Nakupenda* (My Jesus I Love Thee), *Nizidi Yesu Kumjua* (More about Jesus) and *Na Yesu apewe utukufu* (We give all the glory to Jesus). *Ndi Yesu Mukhonyi Wowo* (I gave My Life for Thee), *Niwi uli Musoli* (What Can Wash Away my Sin), *Muhulire, Muhulire Mang'ana Malahi* (When He Cometh), and *Mu Mikhono Cha Yesu* (Safe in the Hands of Jesus). He had even memorized songs from Uganda, for example, *Yesu Mulokozi Wange* (this is in Luganda and it means "Jesus my Saviour").

Exploring the Pauline tent making model

Abraham Khayesi and several of his fellow pastors encouraged their congregations to support the work of God in spreading the gospel. Each church member in a year gave *kipawa* (gift), *injeso* (harvest) of five shillings and budget of five shillings which was to run the executive office in Nyang'ori. Beside these three specific forms of support, they had Sunday offerings, tithes, gifts for the servants of God and volunteer services by members.

To be self-supportive, Abraham and other pastors engaged in some income-generation activities. A few examples are given below:

- Zakayo Imbukule was a coffee farmer;
- Saul Aluda was a coffee farmer;
- Charles Gungu was a maize farmer;
- Abraham Khayesi was a coffee farmer as well as a timber trader;
- Daniel Undusu was a coffee farmer, a school teacher and a dairy farmer; and
- Saul Amuhaya was a coffee farmer.

This approach largely explains why these early pastors did not heavily rely on financial assistance from their congregations. They were able to pay fees for their children and even buy bicycles, which were expensive in those days. They were also able to help members of their congregations and local community who were in need.

The income-generating activities that Abraham Khayesi and Sabeti Shanyisa were involved in were:

- Growing crops (maize, millet, coffee) and keeping livestock. Abraham Khayesi and his brothers inherited pieces of land from their father. They shared the pieces of land among themselves and each used his piece to grow crops;

- Producing and selling timber and bricks. Isaac Shadora recalls that Abraham Khayesi once made about 120 000 bricks, and sold some to Kaimosi Girls High School. Among those who worked on brick-making were Isaac Shadora, Daudi Khuma, Susana Lugarishi, Vitsegwa, Peris, Sarah and Rodah Khasevera. Sabeti Khayesi is remembered for making food for these workers. Some of the people with whom Abraham Khayesi conducted timber trade came from Nandi, Tiriki, Kisii and Maragoli. One of the business friends that family members recall is Jonathan Kipchumba Maiyo and his wife, Salome Menje, from Koitabut. The family also remembers that the timber and bricks were important in constructing educational institutions such as Shamakhokho Primary School and Busali Union schools under the leadership of David Mulindi, former chairman of the Kenya National Union of Teachers;
- Operating a shop, in partnership with their friend, Joseph Masere at Mago market;
- Conducting barter trade in foodstuffs and other basic items. Sabeti Khayesi had friends like Timina from Kiboswa who brought dried fish for her barter trade in exchange for maize. Abraham Khayesi also received salt and kerosene from his friends to barter it for thatching grass for the business community in Nandi;
- Sabeti Shanyisa sold vegetables to teachers in some of the schools near her home. Her children, who attended these schools, helped in taking the vegetables with them to school in the morning, thereby relieving their mother to attend to other domestic chores; and
- Sabeti Shanyisa, with other neighbours and friends such as Timoteo Anduvare, Roseline Anduvare, Rael Aduvaga, Safina Asalache, Elis Akhala, Catherine Omollo and Nicodemus Khaniri formed a Sacco group at Serem market. This benevolent fund was headed by Japheth Ndemaji and a widows' prayer group in the 1980s.

These economic opportunities enabled Abraham Khayesi and his family have new friends from within and without their community. The new friends included Asians at Lunyerere Market, Kalenjins in Nandi and Luo traders from Nyanza. Abraham Khayesi did simple banking by keeping the money in an iron tin or under his bed mattress. When the money increased, Sabeti Shanyisa would transport the money, accompanied by Abraham, to Asian traders based at Lunyerere to keep the money for them. There was no formal banking sector in those days.

It was largely from these additional economic activities that Abraham Khayesi was able to build a brick house in the 1950s. He moved from a grass thatched house to this brick house. He however still built *tsisimba* (huts) for his sons. The initial four-roomed brick house was extended to six rooms. It has also since been renovated twice and still exists.

Giving to Caesar what belongs to him

Abraham Khayesi did not only deal with Church affairs but also with political and administrative issues. He participated in the political affairs of his community and the country. These included:

- Paying taxes. Abraham was very highly respected in the community to the extent that during the head tax collection exercise, the local chiefs and administrators would not come to his home to physically collect the tax. Instead, Abraham honoured his responsibility and would faithfully pay the tax to the government officials, which was kshs. 7.50 for every male who was above 18 years;
- Praying and voting to elect political leaders such as members of parliament and councilors;
- Participating in meetings called by local administrators and visitors to his community;
- Helping to maintain the Shamakhokho-Serem road. He would literally fill the potholes on this road using pieces of bricks from his home;
- Maintaining a good relationship with his workers. The family had several people who helped them with domestic and farm work. Three of the workers whom we remember more or less as part of the family are Joseph Mang'ang'a, Joseph Lunyasi and Charles Akhala; and
- Maintaining peaceful and friendly relationships with his neighbours.

Abraham Khayesi maintained a good relationship with political administrators, right from the village headman (*liguru*) up to the chief. As a matter of fact, he was a friend of these administrators and as children, we often heard him mention and also witnessed him interact with administrators such as Hezron Vuyoywa (chief),

Daniel Amiani (chief), Ezekiel Shibira (assistant chief), Peter Obiero (assistant chief) and Daudi Khuma (village elder).

Fightings and fears within and without

It was not always smooth sailing for Abraham Khayesi, Maria Khanyanji and Sabeti Shanyisa. They did face challenges as they worked as pastors and members of the society. Though they had diversified their economic base, they experienced financial difficulties as their children grew older and joined primary and secondary schools, which required school fees to be paid. They also had heavy family and social responsibilities. In their old age, they did face sickness. For example, Abraham Khayesi had diabetes. Sabeti Shanyisa also had high blood pressure and diabetes. Further, as most parents do, they had to deal with growing children, some of whom sought their own independence and even went against the principles that their parents stood for.

One particular challenge that would have ruined their faith came when a section of the Virembe congregation turned against Abraham Khayesi in 1967, alleging that Abraham and Sabeti Khayesi had mismanaged the church funds (although a treasurer was in charge of the funds) and that they had overstayed at Virembe. Another issue that arose at the same time was that some of the younger members at Virembe congregation and generally in a number of congregations, especially those who were teachers by profession, demanded for a better formally educated pastor who could communicate in English instead of the older pastors like Abraham Khayesi, who had only little formal education.

These two issues threw the Virembe congregation into three groups: those who aligned with Abraham Khayesi, a section opposing him and a non-partisan group. The matter was brought to the board of the local PAG church administration that held a meeting with the entire Virembe assembly to discuss the issues. The meeting, chaired by Mark Mugadia, the then PAG local chairman, found no valid grounds for the allegation. A recommendation by the investigating team called for the transfer of Abraham Khayesi to another congregation in view of the opposing group that had threatened to harm him and his family and also insisted on excommunicating him and his family from participating in Virembe PAG Church activities.

Given the strong opposition from a small group of the congregation that went as far as writing a threatening letter to Abraham Khayesi and the need to maintain integrity of faith, Abraham Khayesi and Sabeti Shanyisa requested Nyang'ori mission headquarters for a transfer, which they were granted. They therefore moved to minister at Kapsambo PAG church. As would be expected, Abraham Khayesi and Sabeti Shanyisa were pained to see some of the young people they had brought up in Christian faith turn against them. It is encouraging to note that in the spirit of forgiveness and reconciliation, a few months after this experience and departure, those who had opposed Abraham Khayesi, sought reconciliation and healing of the strained relationship, claiming that they had been misguided by a few members of the congregation. Despite the pain, Abraham Khayesi and Sabeti Shanyisa forgave them, forged friendship, and promoted Christian brotherhood, love and unity in the family, Church and community. It should be noted that a few other older pastors were also transferred.

This challenging development came at a time when Abraham Khayesi was also facing financial constraints following the admission of his son, Zakaria Khadambi, to Nyang'ori Secondary School, and daughter, Marie Khanyanji, to Bunyore Girls Secondary School. Abraham Khayesi sold off some pieces of family land, cattle, the shop at Mago market and his bicycle to meet the cost of secondary school education for the two children. He was not able to pay fees for other children who were either in primary school or had completed primary school and needed to proceed to secondary school (John, Margaret, Painito) or who dropped out of school for some time (Fridah and James). Opportunities opened up later for these children to either train or continue with school (see Chapter 8).

> **Recollection**
>
> *As children, we learnt from the experience of our parents that life has challenges even when one is a believer in God and it is important to face life and its challenges with courage, faith, perseverance, optimism and patience. In particular, our parents reminded us about hard and thorough work, prayer, reading the Bible and faithfully waiting upon God.*

CHAPTER SEVEN
Abraham Khayesi completes his sojourn

The work of Abraham Khayesi covering the period 1967-1973 is presented in this chapter. It is really in retrospect that one notices that these were the closing years of the mission of Abraham Khayesi here on earth.

Kapsambo PAG Church

The transfer of Abraham Khayesi from Virembe PAG Church to Kapsambo PAG Church did not destroy his faith but instead increased it. His relationships and friends also increased. Among the friends he developed while pastoring at Kapsambo PAG Church were Isaya Isweka and his family, who were and are still members of the Friends Quaker Church. A strong friendship developed between the two families of Isaya Isweka and Abraham Khayesi. Their daughters, Marie Khanyanji and Rachel Isweka, became very close friends and still are, following a friendship that they created while attending Bunyore Girls High School.

While still pastoring at Kapsambo, Abraham, Sabeti and a section of the congregation that stood with them during the Virembe crisis, saw the need to start a local church in 1967. The group that joined Abraham Khayesi and Sabeti Shanyisa to found a local worshipping place known initially as Lusiola PAG Church (which later came to be known as Erusui PAG Church) were Hezron Majanga, Ezna Majanga, Hanna Matafali, Esteli Lwova, James Lumala, Belesi Lumala and Rodah Sesi. Actually, Erusui PAG fellowship started holding its meetings in a house in the home of Hezron Majanga before moving to the piece of land that was donated by Abraham Khayesi (see pictures below). The sanctuary has since been developed further from a mud wall to a brick wall building.

Abraham Khayesi gave out a parcel of his land to build Lusiola sanctuary as an outpost for Mungavo PAG Assembly under the pastoral leadership of Saul Aluda and several elders such as Amos Mwakha, Abraham Anjera and James Lumala. This small outpost continued under the leadership of Mungavo Assembly pastors (Saul Aluda, Samuel Adamba, Zablon Shamagovi, Yohana Inyanje, Habil Mushivoji, Jonathan Mugala, Jackton Indimu, Ezekiel Luyali, Joash Kenyani, Samson Munyeti and Moses Nyando) until 2002 when it became an Assembly. Its first pastor as an assembly was Zakaria Khadambi Khayesi, assisted by Patrick Cheti. At the same time, Abraham, Sabeti and their children continued to maintain their Christian love to the Virembe congregation up to date. Some of his children continued to attend primary school at Virembe and some also attended fellowship at Virembe PAG Church. One of his sons, Mark Mugadia, was also a pastor at Virembe PAG Church from 1987 to 1989.

Old Erusui PAG Church Sanctuary

Current Erusui PAG Church Sanctuary

Kapsotik PAG Church

Abraham Khayesi's health continued to deteriorate and the distance to Kapsambo, in most cases riding a bicycle, was becoming difficult for him. He was therefore transferred from Kapsambo PAG to Kapsotik PAG in 1969 where he served up to 1972. It was while he was at Kapsotik that it was discovered that he was diabetic when he got the first serious attack to his health in 1970. He was unable to continue to minister fully. Kapsotik PAG Church secretary, John Mushenye, and church elder, Thomas Imoli, assisted Abraham Khayesi a lot in carrying out pastoral work. Since Abraham could not make it to the Church every Sunday to take care of his flock due to ill health, these two Church leaders took charge of the congregation and updated him regularly on the progress and spiritual state of the congregation until he was able to resume work fully.

There are several occasions when members of the local community of Erusui and Virembe PAG congregations called upon Abraham Khayesi to pray and counsel them over a number of issues. As already noted, Abraham Khayesi served members beyond his official congregation. He gladly provided spiritual services to members of other congregations; this was with the knowledge and approval of their formal spiritual leaders. Christians would bring newly born babies to Abraham Khayesi's home for him to dedicate them to the Lord right in his house. Abraham Khayesi would also be invited to other places in Tiriki, Maragoli, Bunyore, Isukha, Kabras, Bungoma and Nandi to offer prayers and officiate at such functions as weddings, graduation celebrations of young men after circumcision, and ground-breaking for new houses, schools and churches.

Retirement, homestay and struggle with health and life

From 1972, Abraham Khayesi was unable to attend church and minister on Sunday as he increasingly became physically weak. He therefore retired as a pastor in 1972. He, however, continued to fellowship at Erusui PAG Church, an outpost of Mungavo PAG Assembly. His son, Mark Mugadia, who was a pastor in Mombasa took him to Mombasa in 1972 to provide him with better healthcare. Oral sources indicate that while in Mombasa, Abraham Khayesi saw his imminent departure or passing on in a dream or a vision. He is said to have shared this dream or vision with his children (Jeremiah, Mark, Isaac, Wilfas and Margaret, who were then living in Mombasa), and asked Mark to take him back to Tiriki. Painful as it was, Mark obeyed and took his father back to Tiriki in February 1973.

Abraham Khayesi and son, Mark Mugadia, Mombasa, 1973

Whenever Abraham required transport to go to hospital, and this happened several times, a nearby Catholic priest, Johan Meewis, provided assistance. This priest had a white Volkswagen car, and he would always assist, even at night. This priest gave free lifts to many members of the community. His car was indeed a community resource as he helped virtually every community member, irrespective of their denomination, gender and age.

Last hospital visit, death and burial

The last hospital visit for Abraham Khayesi was in mid May 1973 when he was taken seriously ill. Help was sought from Father Meewis, who transported him to Kakamega Provincial General Hospital. His family members, friends, relatives and church members kept on visiting him while he was in hospital. Sabeti Khayesi would visit, in alternate turns with her children. For example, Zakaria Khadambi visited on Saturday 26 May 1973, and it so happened that he was the last family member to share a talk with Abraham Khayesi.

> **Recollection**
>
> *Zakaria Khadambi vividly remembers the discussion he had with our father on 26 May 1973. They talked about the family, with Abraham explaining how he had taken care of each child, right from Jeremiah to Abigail, and what he expected them to do. He ended the talk by instructing Zakaria Khadambi to take care of his mother, Sabeti Shanyisa, and also to inform her to bring him a meal of meat or liver on her next visit to the hospital.*

On Sunday 27 May 1973, Abraham Khayesi died while at Kakamega Provincial Hospital. The information the family received was that Abraham Khayesi had just prayed for a patient who was very sick in the same ward with him a few minutes before he (Abraham Khayesi) went back to his bed and experienced the last health attack. While in hospital, Abraham Khayesi had continued with his work of praying and encouraging other patients. The family learnt that every morning before the doctor conducted ward rounds, Abraham led fellow patients in his ward in singing, sharing the word of God and praying. One of the nurses who attended to Abraham Khayesi while in hospital was a lady he had led to the Lord and baptized in one of his ministries earlier on in life.

Abraham Khayesi's body was brought home from hospital on the same day, 27 May 1973, on a pick-up owned and driven by his brother-in law, Solomon Shavola. His pastor at that time, John Inyanje of PAG Church at Mungavo, many Christians, friends, neighbours and members of the community worked very hard and closely with the family during the funeral and burial arrangements. The kindness of neighbours like Francis Muhiga and Barnabas Ajevi, who freely provided firewood and maize meal for mourners, was overwhelming. John Asalache, the brother to Abraham Khayesi, worked closely with Sabeti Shanyisa, Daniel Mutsi, Khasievera, Church leaders, family members and community members to oversee the funeral, which involved many Christians and members of the public from several parts of Kenya who kept night vigils while singing and preaching. During this period, we heard so many stories about what our father had done in life.

Front line: from left to right: Obiero (assistant chief) and John Asalache (brother to Abraham Khayesi) during the funeral and burial period of Abraham Khayesi

Abraham Khayesi was buried on Wednesday 30 May 1973 at his home in Erusui village. The burial ceremony was presided over and attended by the then national leaders of PAG Kenya; all of them have died since then. They included Charles Gungu (General Superintendent), Mark Kidula (General Secretary) and Shem Irangi (Principal, Pentecostal Bible College at Nyang'ori). Other Pentecostal Mission workers who attended the burial were Iris Scheel (Goibei Mission Station), Isaac Khaguli (PAG evangelist), Saul Aluda, and several pastors, Church members and members of the public. Abel Mushivoji, who has also died, presided over the burial ceremony.

Sowing a seed of faith and hope

Children and community members a few days after the burial of Abraham Khayesi

Recollection

Meshack Kaina, a pastor with PAG Kenya, recalls that Abraham Khayesi had expressed a wish to be buried in a coffin similar to that of his friend and fellow pioneer of PAG fellow, Zakayo Munyasa. Meshack Kaina reports that he and Mungavo PAG Church leadership saw to it that this wish was fulfilled. The coffin was bought from Kisumu.

CHAPTER EIGHT
Sabeti Shanyisa becomes baba and mama

Stepping into the shoes of a big person can be frightening. Society sometimes judges you not on your own abilities but rather in comparison with your predecessor. When Abraham Khayesi passed on, Sabeti Shanyisa had to combine the roles of being a mother and a father to her children as well as delivering on the joint work that she and Abraham Khayesi had been doing in society and Church.

How do we move on from here?

One of the main issues that Sabeti Shanyisa had to tackle immediately was education for her children who had dropped out of school. There were other issues of adjustment to the death of Abraham Khayesi, including maintaining relationships with the Church, the community and the extended family, as it had happened when Abraham Khayesi was alive.

A turning point was realized when both Zakaria Khadambi and Marie Khanyanji completed training and became teachers in 1973 and 1975, respectively. In addition, Margaret Khashindu who had been supported financially by Mark Mugadia for a secretarial course in Mombasa also secured a job at Senende Secondary School. These three young people took on the responsibility of providing basic needs like food and clothes as well as paying school fees for their siblings. This effort saw Painito Ajanga continue with school by going to Form 1 at Bukhungu High School; Fridah Khasikani continued with primary school education at Mungavo Primary School and proceeded to secondary school education at Kaimosi Girls High School, Goibei Girls High School and Lugulu Girls High School; and James Shisigani continued with primary school education at Erusui Boys Primary School and moved on to secondary school education at Nyang'ori Secondary School. Meleckidzedeck Khayesi also completed primary school education at Erusui Boys' Primary School and proceeded to secondary and high school at Kakamega High School and Maseno National School. Abigail Mmbone completed primary school education at Erusui Girls' Primary School and proceeded with secondary school education at Bunyore Girls High School. John Amayi, in 1974, when asked to choose between going back to school and joining a trade, chose the latter; to train as a driver.

The sacrifices made by Zakaria Khadambi, Marie Khanyanji and Margaret Khashindu to pay fees for their siblings meant that they had to forego their personal goals of pursuing higher education as well as their own personal development aspirations. However, Zakaria and Marie still found room to undertake studies as private candidates for the Advanced Level of Secondary Education (A-level) while working and supporting their siblings. Interestingly, both managed to proceed for further studies and attained university education as well as completed other short courses in their careers. It is encouraging to note that the sacrifices made by these three young people provided a basis that saw their siblings complete school, undertake training, get employment and support themselves as well as help other family and community members where possible. All was however not smooth sailing and not all the younger siblings took up responsibilities to the expected level. Nevertheless, each one of them was provided with a basic foundation to build further on. The young Zakaria, Marie and Margaret, in their 20s, built on the model of collaboration, joint effort and responsibility that Abraham Khayesi, Maria Khanyanji and Sabeti Shanyisa had always pursued. These three young people became role models of older siblings taking care of or supporting their younger siblings, and transforming the social and economic situation of a family. In collaboration with Sabeti Shanyisa, they did provide guidance and an overall supportive family environment.

> **Recollection**
>
> *As young siblings, we remember when Zakaria Khadambi bought a small transistor radio and connected it from his cottage to mama's house for the rest of us to be able to listen to news and a few programmes. We remember when Zakaria married Esther in 1973 and Abigail and Melecki enjoyed skipping a rope with her. We also remember when Zakaria and Esther gave birth to their first born son, Evans, in 1974. He became the darling of the entire family and we took turns looking after him and always wanted to take him with us to places. Abigail would dress Evans in a girl's dress. We even gave Evans nicknames such as nyonyi. We do remember how Zakaria, Maria and Margaret looked out for us and checked on our progress, more or less the way a parent would do, including appraising and reprimanding us as their younger siblings whenever the need arose. We fondly and humorously nicknamed Zakaria kijana because he looked young and charming, and presented himself with a good pose, carrying his head high. We did have our own failures and issues as siblings, including some quarrels and disagreements but there has been an overall sense of belonging to a family among the children of Abraham, Maria and Sabeti Khayesi.*

Sowing a seed of faith and hope

Steering a demanding ship

From 1973 up to the time she died in 2008, Sabeti Shanyisa played this double role of being mama and baba, remaining constant in her faith as she continued to encourage and guide the children, praying for all her children, the church and the community. It was not an easy task for her as she had to take care of her children who were going through several stages of growth and at the same time attend to the different ministries that she had in the Church and community. Indeed, as it happens in life, her children experienced and even brought to her challenges and pain as they wrestled with teenage, youth and adult issues. Despite these challenges, she never relaxed on her parental responsibility to train her children to be God-fearing and valuable to themselves and society. She often recited Biblical scriptures and sang her favourite choruses and songs based on Scriptures such as Psalm 23 and John 3:16. She stressed to her children about the need to obey God and parents as well as to persevere and bear good fruit. The children learnt a lot of Christian songs, Biblical verses and sermons from their parents. As days went by, her children got married. Sabeti Shanyisa was always excited when she received news or witnessed the birth of her grandchildren and great grandchildren. She enjoyed receiving them in her house and she would spend many hours chatting with them.

Sabeti Shanyisa stood firm to see to the growth of Erusui PAG Church. One time, the then regional superintendent dispersed the congregation to other churches. Though very sick in 1994, Sabeti Shanyisa made an effort and travelled to Nyang'ori to discuss the issue with the General Superintendent, Shem Irangi, who restored the church status. Sabeti Shanyisa rarely missed to give tithe, offering and other gifts to the Church and church workers. Though virtually all her children gave her financial support, including money for offering, she would often tell visitors to her house that it was Zakaria Khadambi who had given her money to pay offerings and tithe. She often extended invitations for meals to visiting pastors at the local Church. She had also memorized a lot of scriptures and stories from the Bible, which she recited and narrated with ease in her old age whenever someone else started reading the Bible.

Though Sabeti Khayesi was diagnosed with high blood pressure in August 1981 at St. Elizabeth Hospital at Mukumu, she continued with her life activities. Later in 1990, she was diagnosed with diabetes at Friends Hospital in Kaimosi. As time went by, she continued to be treated and monitored, including admission to hospitals whenever need arose. For instance, between 1995 and 2008, she was attended to at Kenyatta National Hospital, Umoja Medical Clinic in Nairobi where she was diagnosed to be having arthritis, Kikuyu Presbyterian Hospital, Spa Medical Clinic in Nyahururu and Friends Hospital at Kaimosi. Her children, daughters-in-law and grandchildren found it a joy to stay with her while she underwent treatment in Nyahururu and Nairobi, though she always talked about her land, bananas, house and the Church in the village in Tiriki.

Even in the midst of health challenges and pain, Sabeti Khayesi remained lively and prayerful. She indeed acknowledged the pain, especially the painful arthritis in her feet, but retained a positive attitude. The children also noted that she easily developed a friendly relationship with the medical staff. For instance, she would often look out and ask for Mr. Amutavi and Mr. Igala, who were members of the medical staff at Friends Hospital in Kaimosi. They would talk for a long period of time about her health as well as life in general. She also maintained an excellent relationship with all her children, daughters-in-law, sons-in-law, grandchildren, neighbours, church members and community members.

Sabeti Khayesi (right) celebrates her birthday in 2006

In her later days, she would still insist on picking up a piece of paper and a pen to write letters to her children living or working in far places as well as to her siblings and friends. One of the major lessons Sabeti Shanyisa continued to insist on to her children,

Sowing a seed of faith and hope

grandchildren and friends was to avoid over-reliance on assistance and handouts. Instead, she urged them to learn to use their hands to earn a living. Even when Sabeti Shanyisa was unable to go and cultivate on the farm, she insisted on visiting and seeing to it that the farm was cultivated and planted with crops. She would provide the seeds and even pay workers to plant the crops for her on her farm.

Sabeti Shanyisa (first from left, front row) celebrates her last Christmas with family members and friends in 2007

Sabeti Shanyisa dies

On 10 October 2008, Sabeti Shanyisa was taken seriously ill and admitted at Friends Hospital at Kaimosi for treatment. She had a congested chest, which the hospital treated her for, in addition to attending to high blood pressure and diabetes. She improved, was discharged and returned to her home on 15 October 2008. She continued to improve until the night of 16 October 2008 when her condition deteriorated. While being taken care of at her home, she died on 17 October 2008 at 4:00 am in the company of her daughters-in-law, Esther Khadambi and Florence Ajanga, and daughter, Margaret Khashindu. The three reported that Sabeti Shanyisa had passed on peacefully, singing, *Cha kutumaini sina* ("My hope is built on nothing less"), a song we learnt that she persistently sang and hummed in her last week here on earth.

Her body was preserved at Mukumu Hospital to allow family members, relatives and friends to attend the burial. Mama Sabeti was buried by Samson Munyeti, a pastor with PAG (K), on Saturday 25 October 2008 at her home in Erusui village in Tiriki. The funeral service was presided over by the PAG (K) Executive and Mungavo District offices jointly, including the then national PAG (Kenya) General Secretary, John Juma, Pentecostal Bible College Principal, Ganira, and many leaders of PAG (Kenya), religious communities, learning institutions (schools, colleges and universities) and the society. It was a fairly large funeral meeting, attended by many people. Paul Magoti was the pastor of Erusui PAG congregation at the time Sabeti Khayesi passed. He provided spiritual care to her when she was sick and led the local congregation in ensuring that their member was respectfully buried.

The funeral sermon was delivered by David Omalla. All in all, the mourning period was characterised by praises and statements about the excellent work of faith and service that Sabeti Shanyisa and Abraham Khayesi had provided to the community. Her children were supported and comforted by many members of the extended family, church members, community and friends. The key points emphasized about Sabeti Shanyisa through songs, speeches, dirges and sermons, and which were pointed out as lessons for society, were as follows (see also Box 8.1):

- the importance of remaining faithful to God at all times;
- being hospitable;
- being prayerful;
- being a pillar of Christianity in Tiriki;
- being patient;
- value of hard work; and
- the importance of being a loving mother.

Box 8.1
A great African mother

Today we are paying our last respects to a great African Mother

An African Mother who saw beyond the valleys, hills, lakes and plains

An African Mother whose spirits were not dampened by the hardships of the day

An African mother who never showed fatigue

An African mother who represented the true vision of Africa

One maternity after another, she brought forth an entire family which is spread all over Kenya, Africa and the rest of the world.

She was a link between each one of her children and each of the children has become a link to many other God's Children drawn from all over the world

By being a bridge, she taught her children to serve as bridges all over the world

She was a great teacher

Her lessons were great

By teaching her children the first step, she taught them to make great journeys

She taught her children to love and their love is spread all over the world

She taught her children humility, and through humility they are bringing change not only in this village but in villages in many parts of Kenya, and the rest of the world

She taught her children the value of wisdom and her children are spreading wisdom to the rest of world.

She taught her children to share and today they are sharing love with many countless world's children

She taught her children hope and faith and by faith they travel and work in many parts of the world.

She taught her children to shine a light and each one of them is shining a light wherever they are.

Let's keep the Spirit of our great African Mother by keeping her great lessons.

Shining the Light wherever we go!

REST HER SOUL IN PEACE AND LET PERPETUAL LIGHT SHINE ON HER, AMEN.

Written by Mary Njeri Kinyanjui and read by Ezekiel Alembi at Sabeti Shanyisa's funeral service on 25 October 2008.

Yes, life has to go on

The Khayesi family went through the process of adjusting to the departure of Sabeti Shanyisa. For the first time in our lives, we celebrated the Christmas of 25 December 2008 without any of our parents. We wrote e-mails and notes to each other, talked on phone, visited and met together, reached out to each other and continued to build on the foundation our parents had laid for us. The quotations in Box 8.2 below reflect some of the experiences and reflections we went through as we sought to come to terms with the reality of death and had to accept that Sabeti Shanyisa had departed and gone ahead of us.

Box 8.2

Precious memories

"Sometimes I find it difficult to believe that Mama is not here, but I have to remind myself that indeed she went to the Home she often sang of - "Lwakhudukha Mwigulu; Lilava lidukhu liu vuyanzi..." and "Mwigulu yo shikhwakhasevulane inyinga ya khujerera..." (Marie Khanyanji, 8 November 2009).

"We were at home (Abigail, Margaret, Painito and I) to bury Walter Choka and review our grieving of Mama Sabeti at her house. When we sat there today morning, she was not at the places she sat. We now know mama is gone to be with Jesus" (Zakaria Khadambi, 24 November 2008).

"......memories of when your mother was in Nairobi and I had come to visit and I had a great time with her. She would actually call me to the bedroom and start singing. I would join her in some verses and then she would proceed alone to the very end because she knew all verses in most of the good oldies songs" (Jessica Omalla, 5 December 2008).

"She was always there preparing us for the X-mas,

With encouraging words and deeds, she provided to her best at least a good meal,

Like chicks-she made sure we are satisfied.

Yes, we loved her but no more with us this X-mas,

Remembering singing *Yesu Yivulwa* without her this time round

That white dress as she conducted the women X-mas choir,

Then *Vaana vali hena khwenyanga khuli shikhulia*

> Oh, God loved her more than we did,
>
> I hope and believe we shall all share X-mas with her
>
> Her spirit and deeds still linger on in our hearts...
>
> She fought a good fight.
>
> MAMA SABETI SHANYISA.....Merry X-Mas "(Painito Ajanga, 25 December 2008).
>
> "She could not be found anywhere on this world on her 84th birthday
>
> In her small house and under the Cyprus tree in front of her house where she never missed in person she is not found
>
> Fresh in my mind rings the hour of 4 am of 17 October when on my phone I read the message, 'Mama has rested', from my sister Marie
>
> Then I realised that a dear great friend in the Lord has gone
>
> Her teachings, encouragement, singing, laughing and that nice smile I remember yet miss them
>
> The big crowd that mourned her....
>
> On this x-mas day, tears are rolling down my cheeks in my bed
>
> A friend rested in Christ dearly missed
>
> Glory be to God
>
> Pray with me" (Abigail Mmbone Stingo, 25 December 2008)

Marie Khanyanji received a surprising e-mail on 25 December 2008 from a devotional group she communicates with. The text is presented in Box 8.3 below.

Box 8.3

My First Christmas in Heaven

I see the countless
Christmas trees
around the world below
With tiny lights, like Heaven's stars,
reflecting on the snow.

The sight is so spectacular
please wipe away the tear
For I am spending Christmas with
Jesus Christ this year.

I hear the many Christmas songs
that people hold so dear
But the sounds of music can't compare
with the Christmas choir up here.

I have no words to tell you,
the joy their voices bring,
For it is beyond description,
to hear the angels sing.

I know how much you miss me,
I see the pain inside your heart.
But I am not so far away,
We really aren't apart.

So be happy for me, dear ones,
You know I hold you dear.
And be glad I'm spending Christmas
with Jesus Christ this year.

I sent you each a special gift,
from my heavenly home above.
I sent you each a memory
of my undying love.

> After all, love is a gift more precious
> than pure gold.
> was always most important
> the stories Jesus told.
>
> Please love and keep each other,
> my Father said to do.
> I can't count the blessing or love
> has for each of you.
>
> So have a Merry Christmas and
> Wipe away that tear
> Remember, I am spending Christmas with
> Jesus Christ this year
>
> Source: e-mail received by Marie Khayesi, on 25 December 2008 (available at: http://www.angelfire.com/co4/grumpynam/jessi/christmas.html).

The Khayesi family was barely through with mourning the passing on of Sabeti Shanyisa when one of their brothers, John Amayi, passed on in June 2009. Again, we reached out and comforted one another as we attended to his funeral and burial, with great support from extended family, relatives, the community and friends. In August 2015, another Khayesi family member, Ajanga Khayesi, passed on. Again, we reached out and comforted one another as we attended to his funeral and burial, with great support from extended family, relatives, the community and friends.

CHAPTER NINE
Lest we forget: continuing to sow a seed of faith and hope

A refrain that generally runs in the history of many nations, communities and initiatives has to do with how subsequent generations either failed or succeeded in building on the achievements of the generations before them. The author of Ecclesiastes highlights an important issue when he states that a man who has toiled with wisdom, knowledge and skill may leave all he has produced to be enjoyed by a man who did not toil for it (Ecclesiastes 2: 20-21). The problem is not so much with the enjoyment but with failing to be a good steward of the heritage bestowed on the new generation by the old generation. Whereas Paul is confident about his ending, "I have fought the good fight, I have finished the race, I have kept the faith. Henceforth there is laid up for me the crown of righteousness, which the Lord, the righteous judge, will award to me on that Day, and not only to me but also to all who have loved his appearing" (2 Timothy 4: 7-8), he was still concerned about how people were building on the foundation he had helped to lay (1 Corinthians 1: 10-23). We have often heard a statement to the effect that the stars of yester years can be shocked back to death if they woke up to see some of the things being done on what they had laboured very hard on. Some people have even said that these stars could be turning in their graves when they see how the present generation sometimes goes too far from the ideals these stars stood for.

Learning about our history is useful in knowing and understanding the processes, circumstances and people who have shaped and continued to influence our present life. While some people may treat such historical knowledge as an end in itself, others may use it as a motivation to continue developing further the initiatives that have been put in place by those who have gone before them. Indeed, Abraham Khayesi, Maria Khanyanji and Sabeti Shanyisa did not only plant a seed but also watered and harvested some of it. The question to constantly reflect on and act upon by the current and future generations is: "Have we as family members, the community and the Church built well on these efforts?" While this question requires long-term engagement, this chapter provides some emerging direction that is likely to contribute positively or negatively to the building on the foundation that has been laid.

The Khayesi family

The Khayesi family has continued to grow. The children who were very young at the time of their father's death are now adults. Some have married and others are working. We have learnt that while it is an honour to be the children of such an achiever as Abraham Khayesi, this identity comes with very high expectation from society. We have also learnt that while some children are able to continue to uphold this belonging with respect and devotion to the values our parents stood for, others are not. An interesting problem arises here with regard to these two possible trends among the children. Society tends to judge children of achievers in relation to the ability or performance of their parents and not so much with regard to the struggles and challenges of growth that these children face in their lives as individuals. While I always wish that current and future generations build on the foundation laid, I would plead with society to accommodate and support those who are struggling to live to the ideals their parents stood for instead of judging them too harshly without listening to the struggles such children go through. I am making this plea from practical experience in our family. I know that as sons and daughters, we desire to live to the ideals of our parents but we are human and have had to face the world within the context of our experiences and struggles as teenagers, young adults, professionals and members of the community. This process is unique to each individual child and we can all attest to the fact that we do make mistakes and wrong choices as much as we also make right choices and decisions.

Three of the children of Abraham Khayesi became pastors with PAG (K). They are Mark Mugadia, Wilfas Vutembeshe and Zakaria Khadambi. Two grandsons, Zephaniah Mmaitsi (Redeemed Church) and Abraham Khayesi (Deliverance Church) are also pastors. Most of the grandchildren of Abraham Khayesi, Maria Khanyanji and Sabeti Shanyisa are still pursuing formal education. Some of the grandchildren are married and have children, for example, Mary Mbakaya, Emmy Khadambi, Johnston Khasi, Ezekiel Jengo, Nelson Shadora and Evans Khayesi. Some of the children, daughters-in-law and sons-in-law to Abraham Khayesi have since died: Jonah Mmaitsi, Mark Mugadia, William Lugondi, Jeremiah Khadambi, James Shisigani, John Amayi, Peris Lumedwa, Sarah Adolwa, Debla Khasoha, Josephine Amayi and Painito Ajanga. The number of grandchildren and great grandchildren is also increasing.

Sowing a seed of faith and hope

*Four of the sons of Abraham Khayesi with their cousin in 2006
L to R: Musa Muchera (cousin), Jeremiah Khadambi, Zakaria Khadambi, Meleckidzedeck Khayesi and Isaac Shadora*

Taken together, the children, grandchildren and great grandchildren of Abraham, Maria and Sabeti Khayesi continue to pursue in varying degrees the virtues and values of working hard, faith in God, serving society and bearing fruits. While some were or are formally employed as teachers, secretaries, clerks, civil servants and nurses, others are self-employed, operating small businesses. One of the family members, Isaac Shadora, worked as a soldier with the Kenya Navy, retired and later worked as a clerk with Kaimosi Teachers' College. Several are church members, with some holding or having held some leadership roles such as church secretaries, women's leaders and Sunday school teachers or leaders.

Sabeti Shanyisa with her granddaughter (Branice Liani, left) and daughter (Abigail Mmbone, right)

Below is a brief summary on each child:

- Jeremiah Khadambi attended Virembe, Mungavo, Goibei and Nyang'ori primary and intermediate schools, completing Standard Eight at Nyang'ori Intermediate School. He trained as a teacher at Kaimosi Teachers' College at grade Teacher 4 (T4). He first worked as a primary school teacher, and then trained again and worked as a police officer, before changing to the position of a secretary for British Petroleum Company and Smith Mackenzie several years while based in Mombasa. He retired in 1983 and settled in Mpeketoni at the Kenyan coast as a farmer. While living in Mpeketoni, he was also a political party leader and a village elder. He moved back from Mpeketoni to Erusui, his village home, in 1998. He married Rebecca Malina Jagona in 1947. The two had six children, three boys and eight girls: Walter, Emmy, Anusu, Florah, Aggrey and Edith. He died on 18 November 2007 at the age of 80 years, leaving behind his wife, Rebecca Malina, and a total of 35 children, grand-children and great grand-children. He was buried at his home in Erusui village in Tiriki. Rebecca Malina, fondly called 'Mama Njugu', died on 15 January 2017 and was buried on 21 January 2017 at her home in Erusai village.

- Debla Khasoha completed Standard Four and married Jonah Mmaitsi. The two migrated from Tiriki to Lugari. Jonah Mmaitsi passed on in 1978 following a road traffic crash along Eldoret-

Webuye road and Debla Khasoha died on 2 December 2005. They have left behind 6 children, all of them grown up and married and/or working: Samuel, Ezekiel, Phineas, Zephaniah, Mary and Linet.

- Mark Mugadia completed Standard Six at Goibei Primary School. He trained and worked as a police officer in Kitale, Laikipia, Nairobi Industrial Area and Nakuru. He voluntarily resigned as a police officer and joined Nyang'ori Pentecostal Bible College to train as a pastor, responding to God's calling. Following this training, he worked as a pastor with PAG (Kenya) in Tiriki, Mombasa, Nakuru, Nyahururu, Kapsabet, Nandi Hills, Kericho and Kitale. In all these places outside Tiriki, he held the position of District Superintendent, in addition to pastoring assemblies. He died on 10 September 1993, leaving behind a widow, Keziah, who died on 25 February 1999. The two had 10 children. Four have died and six are still alive, working and/or married: Mary, Johnstone, Ruth, Femina, Ruth, Jemimah, Ajanga, Efa, Asheri, Susan and Lydia. Mark was a good singer and peacemaker. While pastoring in Mombasa in the 1970s, Mark used to conduct evening devotions on radio.
- Sarah Adolwa completed primary school. She married Otundo. Sarah had five children: Mary Khanyanji, Livingstone Khasika, Alice Ayuma, Christopher Khayesi and Zedekiah Cheptuya. Both Sarah and Otundo have died.
- Peris Lumedwa completed primary school. She married Daniel Chweya. The two had five children: Rael Ayuma (deceased), Mary Khanyanji, Reuben Yida, Abraham Khayesi and Wainita Musonye. Peris died on 28 December 1980. Chweya has also since died.
- William Lugondi completed Standard Four. He worked as a guard in a security firm. He married his first wife known as Eznah Khalumba. The two divorced. He married his second wife with whom he had two children. One of the children known as Abraham Khayesi died. His other child known as Solomon Andambi is still alive. William died in March 1994.
- Isaac Shadora attended Shamakhokho Primary School and completed Standard Eight. He worked in the Kenya Navy as a sailor at the rank of Senior Private in the period 1966-1972. He married Christina Kavukane in December 1967. Following retirement from the Kenya Navy, he worked as a clerk at

Kaimosi Teachers' Training College. He was the Church Secretary for Virembe PAG Church for 24 years. Later, he worked as an evangelist and studied for a Bible course diploma by correspondence with Bible Way Correspondence School. Isaac and Christina have three children: Nelson Juma, Hiram Khayesi and Mary Khanyanji. One of their children passed on at birth.

- Rabecca Khajeha completed Standard Eight. She married Harun Kajeha. The two had one child. They separated and she remarried Bonifes Wanyonyi, with whom she had two children: Wycliffe and Pauline. Rabecca currently lives in Saosi village, near Mungavo.
- Wilfas Vudembeshe attended Virembe Primary School and completed Standard Eight. He worked as an untrained teacher, a factory employee, a plantation worker and a security guard. He later trained as a pastor and is presently engaged in pastoral work with PAG (K). He married Sevenzia Khavere in 1971. The two have seven children: Rose Shiteshe, Mary Khanyanji, Kennedy Khayesi, Miriam Lumedwa, Stephen Asalache, Cornelius Muchera and Josephine Khajeha.
- Zakaria Khadambi attended Virembe and Mungavo Primary Schools. He also attended Nyang'ori Secondary School and completed Form Four and trained as a teacher at St. Marks Teachers' Training College. He worked as a primary school teacher and headmaster in several schools in Western Kenya. He studied for A-level as a private candidate while working as a teacher and passed well. He completed a Bachelor of Education degree at Kenyatta University in 1988 and worked as a college tutor at Eregi Teachers' Training College. He changed from teaching to work as a curriculum developer for Christian Religious Education with Christain Churches Educational Association and Kenya Institute of Education. He also trained as a pastor and was appointed as a pastor with PAG (K), retiring in 2014. In addition, he trained as a writer and consultant and has conducted several assignments related to political elections, learning material preparation, book writing, civil society and chaplaincy at Baraton College. In 2004, he created a faith-based organisation known as Erusui Kenya Special Ministries, which he currently heads. He married Esther Khavugwi. They have seven children: Evans, Erick, Jacqueline, Branice, Chungani, Fitri and Elizabeth.

- John Amayi attended Virembe and Mungavo Primary Schools, completing Standard Seven in 1969 at Mungavo Primary School. He worked as a petrol station attendant, a bus conductor, tailor and a farmer. He was a scribe to Abraham Khayesi when the latter prepared his life story in 1971. He dictated his story as John Amayi wrote it down. John was a Church usher at Virembe PAG Church. He married Josephine, who passed on in 2008. John had seven children, four died and three survived. John Amayi died on 9 June 2009 at the age of 58, leaving behind three children: Reva, Khayesi and Shanyisa.
- Marie Khanyanji attended Virembe and Mungavo Primary Schools, proceeded to Bunyore Girls High School where she completed Form Four. She trained and worked as a secondary school teacher, a primary school teacher and a teacher' training college tutor. She studied for A-level as a private candidate and passed. She completed a Bachelor of Education degree at Kenyatta University in 1989 and worked as a college tutor and a university librarian. She completed a Master of Library Information Studies (LIS) degree at Kenyatta University in 1996. She attained her PhD degree at University of South Africa (UNISA) in 2010. She worked as a lecturer at Egerton University. She had one son, Rodney Asilla. She died on 22 March, 2019.
- Margaret Khashindu attended Mungavo Primary School and completed Standard Seven. She trained as a secretary. She worked as a secretary at Senende Secondary School and as a small-scale business entrepreneur. She is currently running a small scale firewood business in Tiriki.
- Painito Ajanga attended Virembe, Kaimosi Demonstration and Shamakhokho Primary Schools. He then did his secondary education at Bukhungu and Senende Secondary Schools. He trained as a teacher at Eregi Teachers' Training College, graduating with Primary One (P1) grade. He worked as a primary school teacher in Kakamega, Mombasa and Kisumu districts. In addition, he was a self-educated journalist. He married Florence Nafula Oduor in 1990. The two had three children. One child died and there are two who survived, Elizabeth Shanyisa and Bildad Khayesi. Painito Ajanga died on 29 August 2015, at the age of 59.

- Fridah Khasigani attended Virembe Primary and Mungavo Primary Schools. She joined Kaimosi Girls High School and later completed Fourth form at Lugulu Girls High School. She trained at Christian Industrial Training College in Kisumu as a secretary. She worked at Eregi Teachers' Training college and Friends' School Kaimosi and currently she is working at Laikipia University. She has one daughter, Elizabeth Shanyisa.
- James Shisigani attended Virembe, Shamakhokho and Erusui Boys' primary schools. He completed Form Four at Nyang'ori Secondary School in 1980. After completing secondary education, he worked with 3M in Nairobi. He trained as a primary school teacher at the level of P1 at Eregi Teachers' College in 1983-1985. He worked as a primary school teacher in the following schools: Madeya, Erusui Girls, Mungavo and Shamakhokho and others. He sat for Kenya Advanced Certificate of Education (A-level) examinations as a private candidate in 1986. He married Naomi Khavaya and the two had five children: Getrine, Modline, Lidembu, Brenda and Fidelia. Lidembu passed on in childhood. James Shisigani died on 2 June 2008.
- Meleckidzedeck Khayesi attended Erusui Nursery School, Virembe and Erusui Boys' primary schools, Kakamega High School where he completed Form Four and Maseno National School where he completed Form Six. He completed a Bachelor of Education degree at Kenyatta University in 1988. He worked as a secondary school teacher at Kolanya High School and Njumbi High School, completed both MA and PhD degrees at Kenyatta University, where he also worked as a lecturer up to 2002. He is currently an international civil servant with the World Health Organization, Geneva, Switzerland. He married Jane Nyakecho Omalla on 17 December 1994. The two have two children: David Khayesi and Zipporah Shanyisa.
- Abigail Mmbone attended Erusui Nursery School, Virembe and Erusui Girls' primary schools, Bunyore Girls High School where she completed Form Four. She trained as a primary school teacher at Kamwenja Teachers' College. She has taught

Sowing a seed of faith and hope

in several primary schools in Western and Rift Valley Provinces. She married Reuben Stingo and the two have four children: Erick Ambei, Seth Khayesi, Ryan Itambo and Pelogia Shanyisa.

Part of the Khayesi family celebrating the first day of the New Year in 2016

Pentecostal Assemblies of God (Kenya)

The work of PAG has continued to grow. The PAG church in Kenya currently has 3,500 assemblies with an equal number of pastors. The entire PAG Kenya fellowship has about 4,000, 000 members.

Virembe PAG Church

This congregation currently has about 500 members. Since 1968, its pastors have tended to stay for shorter periods of time as follows:

Pastor	Year
Jafetha Inonda	1968 - 1969
Safania Lilechi	1969 - 1970
Ezekiel Lisitsi	1970 - 1971
Mark Khejeri	1972 - 1973
Joshua Makhulungu	1974 - 1975
Daudi Bulemi	1975 - 1976
Ezekiel Lisitsi	1977 - 1978
Zablon Shamagovi	1979 -1983

Benjamin Sangale	1983 (1 month)
Mark Mugadia	1984 -1985
Habil Mushivoji	1985 - 1986
Samuel Mayavi	1986 - 1987
Mark Mugadia	1987 - 1989
Paul Azihemba	1990 -1991
Peter Javusiono	1991 - 1992
Andrea Mwinyisi	1992 - 1993
Herman Ulira	1993 - 1994
Paul Matasi	1994 - 1995
Tom Wali	1995 - 1996
Moses Hyando	1996 - 1999
Samual Mayavi	1999 - 2003
Elijah Khagai	2003 - 2005
Samson Munyeti	2005 - 2007
Amosi Logose	2007 - 2012
Wilfas Shava	2012 - present

The other congregations where Abraham Khayesi pastored are also still operational. Kapsambo PAG Church currently has about 500 members. Kapsotik PAG Church currently has about 450 members. Erusui PAG Church was for a long period of time one of the local congregations of Mungavo PAG Church. In 2002, Erusui PAG Church became an assembly, with its own pastor. The first pastor was Zacharia Khadambi assisted by Cheti. Presently, it has 150 members.

Let us continue to build on the foundation

Abraham Khayesi, Maria Khanyanji and Sabeti Shanyisa contributed in several ways to Christianity, education and the general society. Their specific contributions included:

a. actively spreading Christianity within and beyond their local community, including giving of their time, resources and home for Christian work as well as providing leadership and mentoring many young Christians and new converts. Examples of their mentees or pupils, who later played key roles in the Church and society are Rabeka Benderi, Selina Lulia, Selina Jirongo, Sangale, the Amalembas and Rael Aduvaka;

b. supporting the development of education through collaborating with others to found Virembe primary school, providing materials towards building of schools like Shamakhokho primary school and Busali Union school, taking their children to school, and encouraging parents in the community to take their children to school;
c. participating in farming and entrepreneurial activities to provide for their families and other members of society in need; and
d. providing guidance and counselling to many members of society. There were many young people who looked to them as their role models and always referred to them as *baba* and *mama*. Many boy children in our local community have been named after our father as a sign of respect and honour to the fulfilling work he did. Many family members have also named their children after Abraham Khayesi, Maria Khanyanji and Sabeti Shanyisa, to the extent that we often have to clarify fully which child we are referring to when family members or these children are together.

There are many lessons each one of us can learn from their lives. I do not wish to prescribe what the reader may do but I hope we can all build in one way or another on these positive contributions. As a family, we thank all the ministers of the Gospel, families and individuals that worked and supported Abraham Khayesi, Maria Khanyanji and Sabeti Shanyisa and their children in fighting the good fight of faith. Above all, the Khayesi family expresses gratitude to God for the gift of hardworking and loving parents. The Khayesi family greatly appreciates Abraham Khayesi, Maria Khanyanji and Sabeti Shanyisa for the true love they had for their children, the community, God and the Church. As a family, we hope that we, the community and the Church will build on the foundation that our parents laid, remembering: "For no other foundation can any one lay other than that which is laid, which is Jesus Christ" (I Corinthians 1: 3:11).

References

Achebe, C. 1958. Things Fall Apart. London: William Heinemann Ltd.

Asalache, K. 1967. A Calabash of Life. London: Longmans.

Kavaya, P. 2003. PAG history: The PAG mantle (part one). Tenessi Printing.

Laws of Kenya. 2010. The Constitution of Kenya-2010. Nairobi: International Institute for Legislative Affairs.

Manana, F. 2000. Keller, Marion and Otto, 1889 to 1953 1888 to 1942. Dictionary of African Christian Biography (http://www.dacb.org/stories/tanzania/keller_marion,otto.html, accessed 10 January 2013).

Manana, F. 2014. Iris Scheel. Dictionary of African ChristianBiography (http://www.dacb.org/stories/kenya/scheel_iris.html, accessed 11 January 2014).

Mbiti, J. 1961. African religions and philosophy. London: Heinemann.

McGee, G. B. 2005. William J. Seymour and the Azusa street revival (http://www.ag.org/enrichmentjournal/199904/026_azusa.cfm, accessed 25 May 2005).

Ngugi wa Thiong'o. 1965. The River Between. London: Heinemann Educational Books.

p'Bitek, O. 1966. Song of Lawino and Song of Ocol. Nairobi: Heinemann Educational Books.

Samita, ZW. 1992. Pneumatology in the African Church of the Holy Spirit, Kabras Division, Kakamega District. Unpublished MA Thesis, Kenyatta University, Department of Philosophy and Religious Studies.

Shisanya, C. 1996. The Abanyole lifwa beliefs and rituals: in search of spiritual liberation. Journal of Eastern African Research & Development, 26: 141-155.

Wamue, G.N. 2001. Revisiting our indigenous shrines through Mungiki. African Affairs, 100: 453-467.

Wafula, R.J. 2001. Crossroads of Western Quakerism in Africa. Quaker Theology, Issue No. 5 (http://www.quaker.org/quest/issue5-4.html , accessed 27 December 2012).

www.ingramcontent.com/pod-product-compliance
Lightning Source LLC
Chambersburg PA
CBHW030055170426
43197CB00010B/1532